If You're So Smart

Donald N. McCloskey

If You're
So Smart

The Narrative of Economic Expertise

The University of Chicago Press

Chicago and London

330
M 127

Donald N. McCloskey is John F. Murray Professor of
Economics and professor of history at the University of Iowa.
His books include *The Applied Theory of Price* and
The Rhetoric of Economics.

The University of Chicago Press, Chicago 60637
The University of Chicago Press, Ltd., London
© 1990 by The University of Chicago
All rights reserved. Published 1990
Printed in the United States of America
99 98 97 96 95 94 93 92 91 90   5 4 3 2 1

Library of Congress Cataloging-in-Publication Data

McCloskey, Donald N.
   If you're so smart : the narrative of economic expertise / Donald
N. McCloskey.
      p.   cm.
   Includes bibliographical references.
   ISBN 0-226-55670-0 (alk. paper)
   1. Economics literature.   I. Title.
HB199.M385   1990
330—dc20   90–33041
                                                      CIP

∞ The paper used in this publication meets the minimum
requirements of the American National Standard for Information
Sciences—Permanence of Paper for Printed Library Materials,
ANSI Z39.48–1984.

Contents

Preface

*E*conomists tell stories in their science, which is no complaint. Everyone tells stories, the toddler telling about the scraped knee and the paleontologist telling about the panda's thumb. A story can be good or bad. When it is bad in economics or other fields of expertise it can do damage. In the worst case the storyteller views the story as "stylized facts" or "approximations of the good" or something else free from critical attention. The uncriticized story is not worth living.

The criticism here is literary, showing that economics and other human sciences rely on metaphors and stories, together. The one figure of speech can criticize the other, with better outcomes. Experts who recognized their literary devices would stop selling snake oil and would come back into the conversation of humankind. That is where they belong, back where we can watch them. The recommendation applies to all experts, economic or not. The economist, though, is a hard and rewarding case.

The book started from pieces written over the past few years, to various audiences, but the rewriting aims at the common reader. The Economics Program of the National Science Foundation supported part of the work, and the Manhattan Institute helped by awarding a national fellowship. The Michigan Institute for the Humanities provided a haven in a busy term. My personal debts are too embarrassingly numerous to record in full. The book is written by numberless economists and English professors of my acquaintance. One of the economists, Arjo Klamer of George

Washington University, a colleague at Iowa during the writing, has been unusually helpful, as is his wont. One of the English professors, Thomas Greene of Yale University, deserves special thanks for his astonishing summer course in 1988 on poetry and magic, at the Dartmouth Summer School of Criticism and Theory; it is his breadth of reference, not mine, that is reflected in Chapter 7. I must also thank Douglas Mitchell of the University of Chicago Press and Peter Dougherty of the Free Press, who saw a book and showed me how to extract it. Julie McCarthy of the University of Chicago Press improved the writing. My student Charles Abbott provided me with a list of stories in my own economics textbook, *The Applied Theory of Price*, which otherwise I would have had a hard time seeing.

I thank the following for permission to recast old metal: Routledge to use parts of "Storytelling in Economics," in Christopher Nash and Martin Warner, eds., *Narrative in Culture* (London: Routledge, 1989) in Chapters 1 and 2; Macmillan Press Ltd. to use parts of the articles "Continuity" and "Counterfactuals" in *The New Palgrave: A Dictionary of Economics* (London: Macmillan; New York: Stockton Press, 1987) in Chapter 6; *The American Scholar* to use parts of "The Limits of Expertise: If You're So Smart," 57 (Summer 1988), 393–406 in Chapters 8 and 9; and *The Cato Journal* to use parts of "The Rhetoric of Economic Development," 7 (Spring/Summer 1987), 249–54.

The context for my ruminations has been the Project on Rhetoric of Inquiry, known as "Poroi" (a Greek word meaning "ways and means"). Poroi is a group of one hundred or so professors of law, mathematics, accounting, literature, history, writing, engineering, philosophy, political science, communications, and a few dozen other fields at the University of Iowa and neighboring schools. The professors have gathered every two weeks winter and summer since 1980 to pursue what they call the Rhetoric of Inquiry, scrutinizing a colleague's paper line by precious line. They have discovered in the end something that should have been obvious at the beginning (professors can be slow, held back by learning)—that scientists and scholars, poets and politicians have in common at least the art of argument.

The art of argument has been studied for 2,500 years in "rhetoric," an ancient and latterly dishonored word. Rhetoric says that we can disagree sharply about politics or the balance of evidence, yet can still pause to note the forms of argument and to speak quietly together about improving them. Rhetoric is the art of a democracy and the science of a liberal education, the art and science of good people speaking well.

The book is dedicated to my good, humane, and learned colleagues at the University of Iowa. They and others are telling a new story, a pragmatic one suited to its Midwestern origins, about how honest argument fares among the people, even among the angry and distracted people of the academy.

Introduction

*I*t is pretty clear that an economist, like a poet, uses metaphors. They are called "models." The market for apartments in New York, says the economist, is "just like" a curve on a blackboard. No one has so far seen a literal demand curve floating in the sky above Manhattan. It's a metaphor.

The parallel proposition is not so clear, but is also true. The proposition is that the economist, like a novelist, uses and misuses stories. Once upon a time we were poor, then capitalism flourished, and now as a result we are rich. Some would tell another, anti-capitalist story; but any economist tells stories. Of course fact and logic also come into the economics, in large doses. Economics is a science, and a jolly good one, too. But a serious argument in economics will use metaphors and stories as well—not for ornament or teaching alone but for the very science.

Like other arts and sciences, that is, economics uses the whole rhetorical tetrad: fact, logic, metaphor, and story. Pieces of it are not enough. The allegedly scientific half of the tetrad, the fact and logic, falls short of an adequate economic science, or even a science of rocks or stars. The allegedly humanistic half falls short of an adequate art of economics, or even a criticism of form and color. Scientists and scholars and artists had better be factual and logical. But the point here is that they had also better be literary. The scientists had better devise good metaphors and tell good stories about the first three minutes of the universe or the last three months of the economy. A scientist with only half of the rhetorical tetrad is going to mess up her science.

It is easy to catch economists, as good scientists, in the act of using stories for their science. Outsiders will find this easier to see than the economists will, because the economists are trained to think of themselves as metaphor-makers instead of storytellers. That again is their happy obsession with models of supply and demand sitting up there in the sky.

Economists spend a good deal of time retelling stories that non-economists tell about the economy, such as: Once upon a time the economy seemed to be doing fine but had a secret monetary illness, then the illness broke out, and therefore everyone became poor. And to each other the economists tell other stories: Once upon a time there was a hog market out of equilibrium, then the sellers lowered the price, and as a result the market got back into equilibrium. Once upon a time the government cleverly reckoned it would drop taxes to achieve full employment, but the public had anticipated the move, and as a result the smart government was outsmarted. Once upon a time an East Asian country was poor, then it studied hard, saved a lot, and borrowed money and ideas from the rich countries, and therefore became rich itself. These stories are not going to dry up the market for *King Lear* or the New Testament, but anyway they are the stories that economists tell.

Not gods but people tell the stories. The stories are not facts made by nature. The artifice does not make the stories arbitrary; it merely makes them various. A paleontologist is constrained by what in fact happened to life and by what he thinks are relevant logics and metaphors. But nonetheless with the same facts he can tell the story in varied ways, as gradualist or catastrophist, for example, running the movie in dignified slow motion or in comic lurches. In geology the story of plate tectonics was told by disregarded cranks for decades before it became the dominant story. The same sort of thing happens in economics. The variety of stories does not make all the varieties equally good or important, no more than the variety of facts or logics or metaphors makes all of them equally good or important. To criticize the varieties of stories, though, you have to know that they are being told.

Stories can go wrong, which is hardly news. We swim all day in wrong stories told by liars, incompetents, and the self-deluded. In economics the wrong stories take a particularly dangerous form, which I shall call snake oil, the cure-all for what ails you. The customer wants the economist to be an expert forecaster, telling that simplest and most charming of economic stories: Once upon a time there was a newspaper reader who was poor; then she read a column by a wise economist, who for some reason was giving his valuable advice to her and two million other readers; and now as a result she is rich. Or: Once upon a time there was a kingdom with a people who did not like to study, preferring to sniff cocaine and watch videos on MTV; then the king hired an expert social engineer who had done much studying; and then as a result the people became prosperous, without of course having to do anything so painful as studying.

Economic snake oil sells, in other words, because the public wants it. The public wants it because of the fears that magicians and medicine men have always assuaged and because the public does not know the limits on economic storytelling. The economists, even many who do not look to a career in selling snake oil, are disabled by their training from knowing the limits. They do not know they are telling stories and therefore cannot distinguish good stories from bad.

One of the bad stories of modern life, in still other words, has a final scene in which the expert, such as the expert on the interest rate prevailing next month, keeps us warm and happy. The analogy with physical engineering, which recently *has* kept us warm and happy, is hard to resist. The social engineer promises to run the economy or the war or the culture with godlike expertise. But on the whole it is a wrong and naughty story, a wicked fairy tale.

And the tale of expert social engineering is unbelievable, really. It cannot answer the simplest folk skepticism: If You're So Smart, why ain't you rich?

The magical story that economists are asked to tell as advisors to governments or as social philosophers fit at best awkwardly and at worst disastrously with the metaphors they build elsewhere in their science. The metaphors, likewise, crash against sensible stories. Economic metaphors if pushed too far, as a 500-equation model of the American economy can be, produce storytelling nonsense. And stories, such as the story of America's tragic decline from Number One, contradict metaphors of maturity and international specialization that we know to be true. As during the 1960s, the badly used 500-equation metaphor can tempt us into trusting tricky policies rather than wise institutions. As in Britain a century ago, the bad story of America's rise and fall can tempt us into figurative and then literal war with our "competitors."

The literary solution to this literary problem in economic science is to use the stories and metaphors to criticize one another. Each part of the rhetorical tetrad, in other words, places limits on the excesses of the others. If you are fanatical about stories alone or about metaphors alone (or logics or facts alone, to finish it off), you will start saying silly and dangerous things in the other realm. The story of the Aryan Race, to take our century's plainest excess in storytelling, needed criticism. So on a lesser plane of evil did the metaphor of methodical accounting for bodies, hearts, and minds in Vietnam. It is better to be moderately, reasonably committed to the observing of true facts, together with the following of true logic, the telling of true stories, and the constructing of true metaphors, combined. It is boring and moderate but it is true. One part of the tetrad checks the other's rank immoderation. The combination yields truth for science and wisdom for policy.

The comic actor John Cleese says that he wants some day to do a scathing, utterly immoderate skit against immoderation. The argument here is a moderate, pluralist argument against monistic immoderation (most of the good arguments since Plato have been monistic and immoderate). Whether it is scathing or not remains to be seen. The proposal in any case is that economics and other expertise use all the resources of human reasoning, the whole rhetorical tetrad. The immoderation that recommends we narrow ourselves down to one piece of the tetrad has done us wrong. It has led us to build high-rise slums and high interest rate economies, and has been especially damaging since the 1950s.

Since those heady years economics has believed itself narrowed down to fact and logic. It shared then belatedly in the temporary narrowing of Western culture called "positivism" or "modernism" (Booth 1974; Klamer 1987b; the word "modernism" in literature means a unified rather than a "dissociated" sensibility, approximately the opposite of its meaning in other realms; see McGrath 1986, chap. 9). Modernism has roots as deep as Plato and Descartes, but in full-blown form it suits its name. Round about 1920 in the West certain philosophers came suddenly to believe that their whole subject could be narrowed down to an artificial language; certain architects came to believe their whole subject could be narrowed to a cube; certain painters came to believe that their whole subject could be narrowed to a surface. Out of this narrowness was supposed to come insight and certitude.

Insight did come (not certitude, alas). In philosophy after modernism we know more about languages lacking human speakers. In architecture we know more about buildings lacking tops. In painting we know more about pictures lacking depth of field. When news of modernism got out to economics around 1950 it yielded some worthwhile insight, too. In economics after modernism we know more about economic models lacking contact with the world.

On the whole, though, the narrowing did not work very well. The failure of modernism in economics and elsewhere in the culture does not say it was a bad idea to try. And it certainly does not say that we should now abandon fact and logic, surface and cube, and surrender to the Celtic curve and the irrational. We are all very glad to keep whatever we have learned from the Bauhaus or the Vienna Circle or the running of rats. It says merely that we should turn back to the work at hand equipped now with the full tetrad of fact, logic, metaphor, and story.

The modernist experiment in getting along with fewer than all the resources of human reasoning puts one in mind of the Midwestern expression, "a few bricks short of a load." It means cracked, irrational. The modernist program of narrowing down our arguments in the name of rationality was a few bricks short of a load. To admit now that metaphor and story matter also in human reasoning does not entail becoming less rational and less reasonable, dressing in saffron robes or tuning into "New Dimensions." On the contrary it entails becoming more rational and more reasonable, because it puts more of what persuades serious people under the scrutiny of reason. Modernism was rigorous about a tiny part of reasoning and angrily unreasonable about the rest.

Bertrand Russell, the master of modernism in philosophy, was a leading case in point (see Booth 1974). Santayana describes Russell during the First World War exploiting his retentive memory without a check of reason:

This information, though accurate, was necessarily partial, and brought forward in a partisan argument; he couldn't know, he refused to know everything; so that his judgments, nominally based on that partial information, were really inspired by passionate prejudice and were always unfair and sometimes mad. He would say, for instance, that the bishops supported the war because they had money invested in munition works. (1986, 441)

Modernists in philosophy or later in economics could not reason with most of their opponents; on most matters they could only shout and sneer. They would say: You are an unscientific fool if you do not believe that in building downtown Dallas the form should follow the function; or you are an ignorant knave if you do not believe that political science should be reduced to mathematics. We need now after modernism to grow beyond the sneers, getting more rigorous and more reasonable about the arguments, all at once.

Modernism seized the word "science" for its purposes. The word has for a long time been a club with which to beat on arguments the modernists did not wish to hear. English speakers over the past century and a half have used it in a peculiar way, as in British academic usage: arts and sciences, the "arts" of literature and philosophy as against the "sciences" of chemistry and geology. A historical geologist in English is a scientist; a political historian is not. The English usage would puzzle an Italian mother boasting of her studious son, *mio scienziato,* my learned one. Italian and other languages use the science word to mean simply "systematic inquiry" (as do for example French, German, Dutch, Spanish, Swedish, Polish, Hungarian, Turkish, Korean, Hindi, and Tamil). Only English, and only the English of the past century, has made physical and biological science (definition 5b in the old *Oxford English Dictionary* [Oxford 1933]) into, as the *Supplement* (1982; compare OED, 2d ed. 1989) describes it, "the dominant sense in ordinary use." It would be a good idea to claim the word back for reasonable and rigorous argument.

The English and modernist mistake, in other words, is to think of science and literature as Two Cultures. The Two-Cultures talk is not written in the stars, though common enough and encouraged by the deans. A dean of research at a large state university gave a talk a couple of years ago in which she spoke of the humanities as what is left over after the (physical and biological) sciences, and then after them the social sciences, have expended their eloquence. The humanities in her mind are a residuum for the mystical and the ineffable. The dean thought she was being good natured. The bad-natured remarks muttered from each side are worse: that if we mention metaphors we are committed to an arty irrationalism; that if we mention logic we are committed to a scientific autism.

One is tempted to shake them both and say, Get serious. The sciences, such as economics, require supposedly humanistic methods, right in the middle of their sciences; and likewise the arts and humanities require fact and logic, right in the middle of their own sciences. Newton used logic and metaphors; Darwin used facts and stories. Science is literary, requiring metaphors and stories in its daily work, and literature is scientific.

Speaking of a science such as economics in literary terms, of course, inverts a recent and guilt-producing hierarchy. But contrary to the century-long and English-speaking program to demarcate science from the rest of the culture—a strange program when you think of it—science is after all a matter of arguing. The ancient categories of argument are going to apply (for which see Perelman and Olbrechts-Tyteca 1969 [1958]; Perelman 1982; Booth 1974; Kennedy 1984; McKeon 1987; Nelson, Megill, and McCloskey, eds., 1987; Vickers 1988, among many others in the revival of rhetoric).

Stories are to be recognized in a complete psychology (Gergen and Gergen 1986; Bruner 1986); so too in economics after modernism (Klamer, McCloskey, and Solow, eds., 1988). A disciple asks his guru how the earth is supported in space. The guru answers readily, "On the back of a giant turtle." The disciple is at first satisfied, but then thinks of an objection. How is the turtle itself supported? The guru pauses, then replies: "On the back of a giant elephant." Good. But the disciple thinks of another objection. How is the elephant in turn supported? The guru reflects long and hard. Ah: "The first elephant is supported by another elephant, and the next by a next: you see, *it's elephants all the way down.*" Founding science on a turtle of certitude was a poor idea. Science is rhetoric, human argument, all the way down (Campbell 1987; Davis and Hersh 1987; Landau 1987; Bazerman 1987, 1988; Klamer 1987a; Carlston 1987; Galison 1987; Collins 1985).

Even ordinary arguing will sometimes use devices unintelligible to particular outsiders, "special topics" in the vocabulary of ancient rhetoric. Lawyers will use cases known only to themselves, and mathematicians will use special theorems. Any scientific community has its language, not to be dismissed as jargon, and its special topics.

At other points in the argument, though, the lawyers and mathematicians will use devices common to other people, "common topics." The appeal to precedent in law is a common topic, which is of course seen outside the law courts and the law journals. Similarly a mathematician makes daily the appeal to authority; but a non-mathematician makes it daily, too. Part of economics uses special topics. But some of its best arguments are common topics. Economic and other expertise shares human reasoning with other fields.

In my own economics or economic history I have many persuasive reasons for preferring a neoclassical, Chicago-school, free-market, quantitative, and mathematical way of telling the story of British economic decline in the late nineteenth century, say, and linking the story to the recent story of the United States. My Marxist, Austrian, institutionalist, non-Chicago, and non-economist friends sometimes do not like my way, and on this or that point they half persuade me, when I grasp their stories. But until the storytelling in economics and in other sciences is recognized we are going to find it hard to be reasonable. We will not know if we are so smart. And the snake oil, curing all our ills in Washington or Des Moines, will continue to be that deadly, secret poison.

1   Telling Stories Economically

Crabs have big molting glands, which makes them good subjects for studying glands in general (Spaziani et al. 1989). There seem to be at least two ways of understanding crab glands and other things: either by way of a metaphor or by way of a story, through something like a poem or through something like a novel. When a biologist is asked to tell why the molting glands of the crab are located just as they are, he has two possibilities. Either he can call on a model—a metaphor, an analogy—of rationality inside the crab, saying that locating them just *there* will maximize the efficiency of the glands in operation; or he can tell a story, organizing real or hypothetical time, about how crabs with badly located glands will fail. If he is lucky with the modeling metaphors he will discover equations with a simple solution. If he is lucky with the storytelling he will discover a true history of maladapted variety of crabs, showing it dying out. Metaphors and stories, models and histories, subject to the discipline of fact and logic, are the two ways of answering "why."

The metaphorical and the narrative questions answer each other. Suppose the biologist happens first to offer his metaphor, his ideal and hypothetical crab moving bits of its body from here to there in search of the best location for molting glands. The listener, still puzzled, asks, "But why?" The biologist will answer the new question with a story: he says, "The reason why the glands must be located well is that if crabs did a poor job of locating their glands they would die off as time passed." A story answers a model.

But similarly a model answers a story. If the biologist gives the evolutionary story first, and the listener then asks "But why?", the biologist answers now with a metaphor: "The reason why the crabs will die off is that poorly located glands would serve poorly in the emergencies of crab life." The glands would not be well located: that's why.

Among the sciences (in the recent English sense) metaphors dominate physics and stories dominate biology. The two can mix; that people regard metaphors and stories as answering each other will guarantee they do. Gregor Mendel's thinking in the 1860s about genetics was a rare case in biology of unmixed modeling, imagining inheritance to be "just like" the rolling of dice. Many decades later his metaphor was answered by the more usual story-telling, at which point people started believing it. In 1902 W. S. Sutton finally observed homologous pairs of chromosomes in grasshoppers. Sutton answered the question asked to a metaphor— "But *why* does the Mendelian model of genes work?"—with a story: "Because, to begin with, the genes are arranged along pairs of chromosomes, which I have seen acting out their little story of splitting and trading, one half from each parent."

The modes of argument are more closely balanced in economics. An economist explains the success of cotton farming in the South before the Civil War in static, modeling terms (he says: the South in 1860 had a comparative advantage in cotton) or he understands it in dynamic, storytelling terms (he says: the situation in 1860 was a natural selection from earlier successes). The best economics combines the two, the static model and the dynamic story, the economic theory and the economic history. For example, in 1920 the Austrian economist Ludwig von Mises wrote a paper on the impracticality of economic calculation under socialism. (The paper speaks to the late 1980s and the fall of socialism.) It was both a modeling of the ignorance that would plague any attempt in the future to replace the market and a story of the failures of War Communism (Lavoie 1985, 49).

The metaphors in economics and other fields have their own

comparative advantage. (I could use here either an evolutionary story from the history of science or a maximizing model from the sociology or philosophy of science.) Metaphors work best at making predictions of tides in the sea or shortages in markets, simulating out into a counterfactual world. In the seventeenth century the physicists gave up stories in favor of models, giving up the claim to tell in a narrative sense how gravity reached up and pulled things down. It just did, according to thus-and-such an equation; let me show you the model. Similarly an economist will argue that a price control on apartments will yield shortages. Don't ask how it will in sequence. It just will, according to thus-and-such an equation; let me show you the model.

On the other hand storytelling works best at understanding something that has already happened, like the evolution of crabs or the development of the modern corporation. The Darwinian story was notably lacking in models, and therefore in predictions. Mendel's model offered to explain the descent of peas and of man by a metaphor rather than by a story and was neglected for years, while natural selection was telling.

One can therefore talk about the models of economics as metaphors, as its "poetics" (McCloskey 1985a). A metaphor brings "two separate domains into cognitive and emotional relation by using language directly appropriate to the one as a lens for seeing the other" (Black 1962, 236). A story, on the other hand, sets down in chronological order the raw experience of one domain. It is a "presentation of a time-ordered or time-related experience that . . . supplements, re-orders, enhances, or interprets unnarrated life" (Booth 1988, 14). The combination of the two is more ambitious and more humanly satisfying. An allegory combines a metaphor (tortoises and hares are like human competitors) with a story (once upon a time the two raced, then the hare took a rest, then as a result the slow and steady tortoise won the race). Economics as a whole, for example, is an allegory of self-interest.

A story from an economist's life can sketch the poetics of economics at work. Shortly after the Second World War the agricultural economist Theodore Schultz, later to win a Nobel prize for the work, spent a term based at Auburn University in Alabama, interviewing farmers in the neighborhood (Schultz 1988). One day he interviewed an old and poor farm couple and was struck by how contented they seemed. Why are you so contented, he asked, though very poor? They answered: You're wrong, Professor. We're not poor. We've used up our farm to educate four children through college, remaking fertile land and well-stocked pens into knowledge of law and Latin. We are rich.

The parents had told Schultz that the *physical* capital, which economists think they understand, is in some sense just like the *human* capital of education. The children now owned it, and so the parents did, too. Once it had been rail fences and hog pens and mules. Now it was in the children's brains, this human capital. The farm couple *was* rich.

The average economist was willing to accept the discovery of human capital as soon as he understood it, which is in fact how many scientific and scholarly discoveries are received. It was an argument in a metaphor (or if you like: an analogy, a simile, a model). A hog pen, Schultz would say to another economist, is "just like" Latin 101. The other economist would have to admit that there was something to it. Both the hog pen and the Latin instruction are paid for by saving. Both are valuable assets for earning income, understanding "income" to mean, as economists put it, "a stream of satisfaction." Year after year the hog pen and the Latin cause satisfaction to stream out like water from a dam. Both last a long time but finally wear out when the pen falls down and the Latin-learned brain dies. And the one piece of "capital" can be made into the other. An educated farmer, because of his degree in agriculture from Auburn, can get a bank loan to build a hog pen; when his children grow up he can sell off the part of the farm with the hog pen to pay for another term for Junior and Sis up at Auburn, too.

So economists use metaphors in their science, like poets. An economist is a poet / But doesn't know it. The parallel proposition, the theme here, is that the economist is also a novelist and lives happily ever after. As the literary critic Peter Brooks said in *Reading for the Plot:* "Our lives are ceaselessly intertwined with narrative, with the stories that we tell . . . all of which are reworked in that story of our own lives that we narrate to ourselves. . . . We are immersed in narrative" (1985, 3). Or as the historian J. H. Hexter put it, storytelling is "a sort of knowledge we cannot live without" (1986, 8).

Economists have not lived without stories, not ever. Stories, as a working title had it, are "instruments of culture" (Nash and Warner 1989). It is perhaps no accident that economic science and the novel were born at about the same time (compare Brooks 1985, 5). It is perhaps no accident, either, that modernist stories of science flooded in as the sea of faith receded. We live in an age insatiate of stories.

Tell me a story, Dr. Smith. Why of course:

A pension scheme is proposed for the nation, in which "the employer will pay half." It will say in the law and on the worker's salary check that the worker contributes 5 percent of his wages to the pension fund but that the boss contributes the other 5 percent. The example is a leading case in the old debate between lawyers and economists. A law is passed designed (as people say) to have such and such an effect. The lawyerly mind goes only this far. According to the lawyer, under the pension scheme the workers will be 5 percent better off on balance, getting half of their pension free.

No economist, though, will want to leave the story of the pension plan in the first act, the lawyer's and legislator's act of laws designed to split the costs. Her suspicion is always aroused by things said to be free. She will want to go further into the little drama of pensions. She will say: "At the higher cost of labor the bosses will hire fewer workers. In the second act, consequently, the situation created by the law will begin to dissolve. At the old wage but with the pension added, more workers will want to get jobs than the boss wishes to give. Jostling queues will form outside the factory gate. The competition of the workers will drive down wages. By the third and final act a part of the 'boss's' share of the pension costs—maybe even all of it—will sit on the workers themselves, in the form of lower wages. The intent of the law," the economist will conclude with a smirk, "will have been frustrated."

Thus in Chicago when a tax on employment was proposed the reporters asked who would pay the tax. Alderman Thomas Keane (who later went to jail, though not for misappropriation of economics) declared that the City had been careful to draft the law so that only the employers paid it. "The City of Chicago," said Keane, "will never tax the working man." Ah, yes.

Thus again in 1987, when Senator Ted Kennedy proposed a plan for workers and employers to share the cost of health insurance, the newspapers reported Kennedy as estimating "the overall cost at $25 billion—$20 billion paid by employers and $5 billion by workers." Senator Kennedy will never tax the working man. The manager of employee relations at the U.S. Chamber of Commerce (who apparently agreed with Senator Kennedy's economic analysis of where the tax would fall) said, "It is ridiculous to believe that every company . . . can afford to provide such a generous array of health care benefits." The U.S. Chamber of Commerce will never tax the company.

The case illustrates a number of points about economic stories. It illustrates the pleasure economists take in unforeseen consequences, trick endings, a pleasure shared with other social scientists. It illustrates the selection of certain plots for special attention: an accountant or political scientist would want to hear exactly how the pension was funded, because the details of funding, which do not matter in the economist's way of storytelling, might affect the behavior of politicians or businesspeople in the future. It illustrates also the way that in telling their stories economists draw on typical scenes—the queues in front of the factory—and typical metaphors—workers as commodities to be bought and sold.

But most importantly here it illustrates the way stories support economic argument. Since Adam Smith and David Ricardo economists have been addicted to little analytic stories. (The addiction even has a name, "the Ricardian vice.") The economist says, "Yes, I know how the story begins in the first act; but I see dramatic possibilities; I see how events will develop from the situation at the start."

It is not controversial that an economist is a storyteller when she is telling the story of the Federal Reserve Board last year or the story of the industrial revolution in Britain last century. Plainly and routinely, 90 percent of what economists do is such storytelling. Yet even in the other 10 percent, in the part more obviously dominated by models and metaphors, the economist tells stories. Economists tell a lot of stories, and must practice therefore the art of telling.

Continuity and discontinuity, to give an example of the telling in detail, are devices of storytelling. The story of monetary policy over the past few months or the story of modern economic growth can be told as gradualist or catastrophist. How do you decide which is the better story? If stories are one part of economic science, how are they evaluated?

Consider one feature of the master story of modern life, the nature and causes of the wealth of nations. If the British industrial revolution was a "revolution," as it surely was, it happened at some time. There was a discontinuity, a before and after in the story. Various dates have been proposed, down to the famous day and year: such as the ninth of March 1776, when *The Wealth of Nations* provided an ideology for the age; or the five months in 1769 when Watt took out a patent on the high-pressure steam engine and Arkwright on the cotton-spinning water frame; or the first of January 1760, when the furnaces at Carron Ironworks, Stirlingshire were lit.

Such dating has of course an amateur air, part of a bad story. A definite date looks handsome on a plaque or scroll but the precision does not fit well with sophisticated storytelling. The discontinuity is implausibly sharp, drawing attention to minor details. The Great Depression did not start on 24 October 1929; the deregulation of

American banking was not completed with the repeal of laws restricting the payment of interest. The historical economist Nicholas Crafts (1977) has pointed out that the detailed timing of the industrial revolution should not anyway be the thing to be studied, because small beginnings do not come labeled with their probabilities of developing into great revolutions. He is identifying a pitfall in storytelling. The historical economist Joel Mokyr identifies another (1985, 44): rummaging among the possible acorns from which the great oak of the industrial revolution grew "is a bit like studying the history of Jewish dissenters between 50 B.C. and A.D. What we are looking at is the inception of something which was at first insignificant and even bizarre," albeit "destined to change the life of every man and woman in the West."

What is destined or not destined to change our lives will look rather different to each of us. Each historical economist therefore has his or her own dating of the industrial revolution, though varying in persuasiveness. Each sees another discontinuity. Elizabeth Carus-Wilson (1954 [1941], 41) spoke of "an industrial revolution of the 13th century": she found that the fulling mill was "due to scientific discoveries and changes in technique" and "was destined to alter the face of medieval England." A. R. Bridbury (1975, xix–xx) found in the late Middle Ages "a country traveling slowly along the road . . . that [it] traveled so very much more quickly in Adam Smith's day." In the eyes of Marxist writers the sixteenth century was the discontinuity, when capitalism set off into the world to seek its fortune. John U. Nef (1932), no Marxist, believed he saw an industrial revolution in the sixteenth century, centered on coal, though admittedly it slowed in the seventeenth century. A student of the seventeenth century itself, such as D. C. Coleman (1977), finds glimmerings of economic growth even in that disordered age. The most widely accepted period for the industrial revolution is the late eighteenth century, especially the 1760s and 1770s (Mantoux 1961 [1928]; Landes 1965, 1969), but recent students of the matter (Harley 1982; Crafts 1984) have found much to admire in the accomplishments of the early eighteenth century. W. W. Rostow

(1960) placed the "take-off into self-sustained growth" in the last two decades of the eighteenth century, but others have observed that even by 1850 the majority of British people remained in traditional sectors of the economy. And later still there was a second industrial revolution (of chemicals, electricity, and internal combustion) and a third (of electronics and biology).

Wider perspectives are possible, so wide as to encourage seeing continuity instead. Looking at the matter from 1907, Henry Adams could see a "movement from unity into multiplicity, between 1200 and 1900, . . . unbroken in sequence, and rapid in acceleration" (1931 [1906], 498). The principal modern student of the industrial revolution, R. M. Hartwell, appealed for continuity against the jostling throng of dates: "Do we need an *explanation* of the industrial revolution? Could it not be the culmination of a most unspectacular process, the consequence of a long period of economic growth?" (1967 [1965], 78).

Such questions of continuity and discontinuity are asked widely in economics, though sometimes only half consciously. The questions cannot be left to historians. Economics is mainly contemporary history and faces the problem of deciding when a piece of history has been continuous or not. For instance the discontinuity in the growth of big government, as Robert Higgs points out (1987), might be placed when the American institutions of big government were first thought up (1900–1918) or made (1930–45) or expanded (1960–70). Even recent and technical history in economics faces this storytelling problem. When, if ever, did the international alignment of prices and exchange rates break down in the 1970s? When did policy on antitrust alter to favor mergers? When did monetary policy last become expansionary? Where is the break? It is a question of stories.

The question has often been misconstrued as philosophical. The philosophical difficulty was first articulated in the fifth century B.C. by Parmenides and his student Zeno: that if everything is perfectly continuous, change is impossible (Korner 1967). Everything is, so to speak, packed too tightly to move. The economist will recognize the point as analogous to an extreme form of economic equilibrium; the physicist will recognize it as maximum entropy. If human nature doesn't "really" change, then history will be a string of weary announcements that the more things change the more they stay the same. If the economy is "really" in equilibrium all the time, then nothing remains to be done.

The economist and historian Alexander Gerschenkron noted that such a metaphysics would close the book of history (1962a, 12). A history or economics that began with the Parmenidean continuum would never speak. For purposes of social science Gerschenkron rejected the transition from the connectedness of all change to an absence of change. True, if you squint and fit a curve then no economic story looks discontinuous in the mathematical sense; but it is wrong then to deduce that "really" there is no change at all, or that the industrial revolution is a mirage. "Continuity" in the strict mathematical sense must be kept distinct from "continuity" in the storytelling sense.

Economists have often been muddled about this philosophical distinction, drawing surprising ideological implications from it. The great British economist of a century ago, Alfred Marshall, enshrined on the title page of his *Principles of Economics* (1890 and later edition) the motto *natura non facit saltum* (nature does not make a jump; Leibnitz and Linnaeus are early users of the phrase, which appears to date from Jacques Tissot in 1613). Marshall himself seems to have believed that the ability to represent behavior with mathematical curves that do not jump implies that the economic theory called "marginalism" is a good description of human behavior. (Marginalism says that humans calculate how far they should go.) One is less sure that Marshall believed that the lack of jumps in nature (quantum physics was about to make big jumps big news) implies that people should not jump either and should change society only gradually.

Anyway, both implications are commonly drawn and both are non sequiturs. Though both have been attributed to the modern mainstream in American economics, so-called neoclassical economics, neither one is necessary for it. Much bitter controversy has assumed that neoclassical economics depends on smooth curves and in consequence must advocate smooth social policies. There is a peculiar alliance in economics between discrete (jumpy) mathematics and Marxian economics, with its jumpy political program. There is an equally peculiar enthusiasm of some conservative writers for continuities in economic history. Gerschenkron cursed both their houses: the scientific storyteller should study change and continuity "unbothered by the lovers and haters of revolutions who must find themselves playgrounds and battle grounds outside the area of serious scholarship" (1962a, 39).

The main problems of continuity and discontinuity, however, are not solvable in seminars on philosophy. They are practical problems in the rhetoric of measurement and must be solved in the economic or historical workshop. When shall we say that the industrial revolution happened? Gerschenkron himself gave an answer confined to industry, for in common with most economic historians he regarded agriculture and services as laggards in economic growth. "In a number of major countries of Europe. . . . after a lengthy period of fairly low rates of growth came a moment of more or less sudden increase in the rates, which then remained at the accelerated level for a considerable period. That was the period of the great spurt in the respective countries' industrial development. . . . The rates and the margin between them in the 'pre-kink' and the 'post-kink' periods appear to vary depending on the degree of relative backwardness of the country at the time of the acceleration" (1962a [1968, 33–34]).

The level at which such discontinuity is to be observed is at choice. As Gerschenkron remarked, "If the seat of the great spurt lies in the area of manufacturing, it would be inept to try to locate the discontinuity by scrutinizing data on large aggregate magnitudes such as national income. . . . By the time industry has become bulky enough to affect the larger aggregate, the exciting period of the great spurt may well be over" (34–35). Inept, he says. The story would be badly told. In a footnote to these sentences he deals with his bête noire, Walt Whitman Rostow (a stage theorist as an economic historian, one of the first appliers of modern economics to history and, less happily, an advisor to presidents). Rostow's "failure to appreciate this point has detracted greatly from his concept of the take-off [Rostow's set of metaphors about the discontinuity], which in principle is closely related to the concept of the great spurt as developed by this writer."

The point is a good one and applies to all questions of continuity in aggregate economics, or aggregate anything. Small (and exciting) beginnings will be hidden by the mass until well after they have become routine. Recall Crafts and Mokyr on eighteenth-century industry. Mokyr has put it as a matter of arithmetic: if the traditional sector of an economy is growing at a slow 1 percent per annum and starts with 90 percent of output, the modern sector growing at a fast 4 percent per annum will take three-quarters of a century to account for as much as half of output (1985, 5). It's just the arithmetic. We may call it the Weighting Theorem (or the Waiting Theorem, for the wait is long when the weight is small to begin with). There are parallel points to be made elsewhere in economics and in social science generally. In the branch of mathematical economics called growth theory, for instance, as was noticed shortly after its birth, a century of theoretical time is needed in most models for a shift to yield growth of as much as 90 percent of its final, "steady" state. More generally, economists have long recognized the tension between microeconomic explanations and macroeconomic things to be explained. In stable models the small beginnings stay small for a long time.

The point about small beginnings is not confined to economics: sociologists quarrel in the same way, using even the same jargon of micro and macro. The search for discontinuity in an aggregate curve raises the question of the level at which we should do our social thinking, the so-called aggregation problem. It would apply to literary history, too: is Romanticism best studied in Blake or Browning, in its small beginnings or its full career?

Gerschenkron himself, unfortunately, did not answer the storytelling question well by his own standards and was in the end hoist by his own petard. In an important work examining Italian industrial output Gerschenkron placed the "great spurt" in the period 1896–1908 and wished to explain it with the great banks founded about the same time, in the 1890s. Stefano Fenoaltea, fleetingly a student of Gerschenkron (until the student contradicted the master), applied the Weighting Theorem to the case (Fenoaltea, n.d.). Surely, Fenoaltea reasoned, the components of the industrial index—the steel output and the chemical output—are the "real" units of economic analysis. (People talk this way, incidentally, when they want to make a storytelling point but do not want to defend it explicitly. The rhetoric of "reality" is used nowadays by some economists to coerce other economists into giving micro foundation for all of their macroeconomics.) Fenoaltea noted that if the little components started accelerating *before* the great banks appeared, becoming bulky only later, then the banks could not have been the initiating force.

Unhappily, the little components did just this. They spoil Gerschenkron's bank-led story of Italian industrialization: the components accelerated not in the nineties but in the eighties, not after but before the banks made their mark. To paraphrase Gerschenkron on Rostow, by the time the progressive components of industry had become bulky enough to affect the larger aggregate, the exciting period was well over.

Yet the moral is still Gerschenkron's: that continuity and discontinuity are tools "forged by the historian rather than something inherently and invariantly contained in the historical matter. . . . At all times it is the ordering hand of the historian that creates continuities or discontinuities" (1962a, 38). Gerschenkron nodded, but the nodding makes the point. The multiple datings of the industrial revolution make it, too. So does any choice of smoothness or suddenness in economic storytelling.

The point is that history, like economics, to say it again, is a story we tell. Continuity and discontinuity are narrative devices, to be chosen for their storytelling virtues. Niels Bohr said once that "It is wrong to think that the task of physics is to find out how nature is. Physics concerns what we can say about nature" (Moore 1985 [1966], 406). It is *our* say. We can choose to emphasize the continuous: "Abraham begat Isaac; . . . begat . . . begat . . . and Jacob begat Joseph the husband of Mary, of whom was born Jesus." Or the discontinuous: "There was in the days of Herod, the king of Judea; a certain priest named Zacharias." It is the same story, but its continuity or discontinuity is our creation, not God's.

Economists spend a lot of time worrying whether their metaphors—they call them "models"—meet rigorous standards of logic. They worry less whether their stories—they call them "stylized facts," a phrase that makes tiresome trips to the library unnecessary—meet rigorous standards of fact. The choice to have high standards of logic, low standards of fact, and no explicit standards of metaphor and story is itself a rhetorical one. It depends on the audience of economic scientists. If economists become economists by way of the Department of Mathematics, for example, it will not be surprising when they bring along a rhetoric of logic-is-enough; if by way of the Department of History, a rhetoric of facts-are-enough. Few economists become economists by way of the Department of English or of Communications, and so not many know they are telling stories.

2 Plot and Genre in Economics

*A*ny moderately broad conversation like economics, then, will involve the rhetorical tetrad—fact, logic, metaphor, and especially story.

Telling the stories in economics as matters of beginnings, middles, and ends has many attractions. A proper scientific treatment would start with pure plot, breaking 100 economic stories down into their components as the Russian folklorist Vladímir Propp did in 1928 for 100 Russian folk tales (1968 [1928], 19–24). In economics they would be the capitalization-of-Iowa-corn-prices tale, the exit-from-and-entry-to-computer-selling-in-the-1980s tale, the correct-burden-of-the-Kennedy-health-insurance tale, the great-oaks-from-little-acorns-grow tale, and so forth. The tales would then be analyzed into "functions" (Propp's word for actions). And, to Proppize it entirely, one would ask whether the sequences of functions prove to be constant, as they are in Russia.

The task sounds bizarre. But actually economics is too easy a case. It is not hard enough to make it scientifically worthwhile to go searching for structure in economic stories. Economics is already structural, as the linguist Ferdinand de Saussure pointed out long ago (1983 [1916], 79, 113). The actions of an economistic folklore are few: entry, exit, price setting, orders within a firm, purchase, sale, valuation, and a few more. It is indeed this self-consciously structural element that makes economics so irritating to outsiders. Economists say over and over again, "action X is just like action Y"—labor is just like a commodity, slavery is just like capitalization, children are just like refrigerators, and so forth.

The economist's favorite phrase should please literary intellectuals, who look for hidden structure below the surface of things: "underneath it all." Underneath it all, international trade among nations is trade among individuals and can be modeled in the same way. Underneath it all, an inflated price is earned by someone as an inflation wage, leaving average welfare unchanged. Underneath it all, we owe the national debt to ourselves (the people who pay the taxes might wonder about this one). In such a highly structured field, whose principles of storytelling are so well known by the main storytellers, it would be surprising to find as many as thirty-one distinct actions, as Propp found in his 100 Russian folk tales (1968 [1928], 64). He found seven different characters (80). That seems more likely: the early English economist David Ricardo (the one who brought Ricardian vice into the world) got along in his economic tales with three—the worker, the landlord, and the farmer.

Tale-telling in economics follows the less formal constraints of fiction, too. The most important is the sense of an ending, as in the story of the pension scheme. Go all the way to the third act. In notably economic language the Bulgarian-French literary critic Tzvetan Todorov asserted that "the minimal complete plot consists of the transition from one equilibrium to another" (quoted in Prince 1973, 31). Gerald Prince used some ingenious mental experiments with stories and non-stories to formulate a definition of the "minimal story," which has

three conjoined events. The first and third events are stative [such as "John was poor"], the second is active [such as "then John found a pot of gold"]. Furthermore, the third event is the inverse of the first [such as "John was rich"]. . . . The three events are conjoined by conjunctive features in such a way that (a) the first event precedes the second in time and the second precedes the third, and (b) the second event causes the third. (31)

Prince's technique isolates what it is about the tales that we recognize as stories. Is this a story?

A man laughed and a woman sang.

No, it does not feel like one—in the uninstructed sense we learned at our mother's knee (anything of course can be a story after Joyce and Kafka, not to speak of writers of French detective stories). The following sounds more like a story:

John was rich, then he lost a lot of money.

At least it has the claim of sequence or consequence, "then." And it has the inversion of status ("rich . . . poor"). But it doesn't quite make it. Consider:

A man was happy, then he met a woman, then, as a result, he was unhappy.

Right. It feels like a complete story, as "generally and intuitively recognized" (5). Contrast:

John was rich and he traveled a lot, then, as a result, he was very happy.

Something is screwy. What is screwy is that his status is not inverted from what it was.

One can use Prince's examples to construct stories and non-stories in economics. Test the pattern:

Poland was poor, then it adopted capitalism, then as a result it became rich.

The money supply increased this year, then, as a result, productivity last year rose and the business cycle three decades ago peaked.

A few firms existed in chemicals, then they merged, and then only one firm existed.

Britain in the late nineteenth century was capitalistic and rich and powerful.

The pattern is story/non-story/story/non-story.

Stories end in a new state. If the story of the pension scheme ended with a 5 percent gain by the worker the economist says "it is

not an equilibrium." "Not an equilibrium" is the economist's way
of saying that he disputes the ending proposed by some untutored
person. Any descendant of Adam Smith, left or right, by way of
Marx or Marshall or Menger, will be happy to tell you a better
story.

Many of the disagreements inside economics turn on this sense
of an ending. To an eclectic Keynesian, raised on picturesque tales
of economic surprise, the story idea "Oil prices went up, which
caused inflation" is full of meaning, having the merits that stories
are supposed to have. But to a monetarist, raised on the classical
unities of money, it seems incomplete, no story at all, a flop. As the
economist A. C. Harberger likes to say, it doesn't make the economics "sing." It ends too soon, halfway through the second act: a
rise in oil prices without some corresponding fall elsewhere is "not
an equilibrium."

From the other side, the criticism of monetarism by Keynesians
is likewise a criticism of the plot line, complaining of an ill-moti-
vated beginning rather than a premature ending: where on earth
does the money you think is so important come from, and why?
The jargon word is "exogenous": if you start the story in the middle the money will be treated as though it is unrelated to,
exogenous to, the rest of the action, even though it's not.

There is more than prettiness in such matters of plot. There is
moral weight. The historian Hayden White has written that "The
demand for closure in the historical story is a demand . . . for
moral reasoning" (1981, 20). A monetarist is not morally satisfied
until she has pinned the blame on the Federal Reserve. The economist's ending to the pension story says, "Look: you're getting
fooled by the politicians and lawyers if you think that specifying
the 50-50 share in the law will get the workers a 50 percent cheap-
er pension. Wake up; act your age; look beneath the surface;
recognize the dismal ironies of life." Stories impart meaning,
which is to say worth. A *New Yorker* cartoon shows a woman
looking up anxiously from the TV, asking her husband, "Henry, is
there a moral to *our* story?"

The sense of adequacy in storytelling works in the most abstract theory, too. In seminars on mathematical economics a question nearly as common as "Haven't you left off the second subscript?" is "What is your story?" The story of the pension scheme can be put entirely mathematically and metaphorically, as an assertion about where the pension tax falls, speaking of supply and demand curves in equilibrium thus:

$$w^* = - [E_d/(E_d + E_s)]T^*.$$

The mathematics here is so familiar to an economist that he will not need explanation beyond the metaphor. (It says that the tax is shared between demanders of labor and suppliers of labor depending on how sensitive they are to wages.) But in less familiar cases, at the frontier of economic argument, the economist will need an explanation. That is, he will need a story. Like the audience for the biologist explaining molting glands in crabs, at the end of all the mathematics he will ask insistently *why*. In advanced seminars on economics "What is your story?" has become a technical phrase. It is an appeal for a lower level of abstraction, closer to the episodes of human life. It asks for more realism in a fictional sense, more illusion of direct experience. It asks to step closer to the nineteenth-century short story, with its powerful and nonironic sense of Being There.

And of course even the most static and abstract argument in economics, refusing to become storylike and insisting on remaining poetic and metaphorical, is part of "that story of our own lives which we narrate to ourselves." A scholar has a story in which the work in question is an episode. This is why seminars in very abstract and metaphorical fields, such as mathematics and parts of economics, so often begin with "how I came to this subject." The fragment of autobiography gives meaning to it all. You will hear mathematicians complain if a seminar has not been "motivated." The motivation is a story, frequently a mythic history about this part of mathematics or about this speaker. The audience wishes to know why the argument might matter to the speaker and therefore to the audience itself. The story will then have a moral, as all good stories do. Listen, my children, and you shall hear / Of the marketing life of an auctioneer.

Economics-as-story provides a place to stand from which to look at the plots of economics. To repeat, the author must be a novelist or a poet, a user of either a story or a metaphor. But the reader, too, figures in economic thought. A useful distinction has been drawn by the literary critic Louise Rosenblatt (1978) between aesthetic and efferent reading. In efferent reading (from Latin *effero*, I carry off) the reader focuses on what she will carry off from the reading. Efferent reading is supposed to characterize model building and science. Model building and science is supposed to be useful for something outside itself. In aesthetic reading, by contrast, the reader focuses on her experience at the time of reading. The aesthetic is supposed to characterize storytelling and art.

Yet an aesthetic reading of a scientific text commonly clinches the argument. The feeling "Yes: this is right" in the last stanza of Yeats' poem "Among School Children" resembles the feeling that comes from the ancient proof that the square root of 2 cannot be expressed as the ratio of two whole numbers. Rosenblatt supposes that "To adopt an aesthetic stance . . . toward the directions for constructing a radio is possible, but would usually be very unrewarding" (34). Well, usually. Yet the computer repairman takes an aesthetic attitude toward the schematics for a Murrow computer: "A nice little machine," he says, and smiles, and is brought to this or that solution. The Nobelian physicist Steven Weinberg argues that aesthetic readings govern the spending of millions of dollars in research money (1983). His own theory, ugly before some new results arrived, came to be reckoned beautiful enough to test with $40 million (four times the National Science Foundation's budget for all of economics, by the way). The pleasure of the text is sometimes its meaning, even in science.

Rosenblatt anticipates such an argument, noting that theories of literature that do not stress the reader's role are left puzzled by pleasurable nonfiction, such as *The Decline and Fall of the Roman*

Empire or, one might add, the best applied economics, as that of Ronald Coase or A. C. Harberger. The reader's response gives a way of keeping track of the aesthetic readings when they matter. The naive theory of scientific reading asserts that they never do.

The telling of artful stories has its customs, and these too may be brought to economics. Take for instance the bare notion of genre, that is, of types of literary production, with their histories and their relations to each other. Poets have epic and lyric, pastoral and narrative. The scientific report is itself a genre, whose conventions have changed from time to time. Kepler wrote in an autobiographical style, spilling his laboratory notes with all their false trails onto the page; Galileo wrote urbane little dramas. It was Newton, in other ways also an unattractive man, who insisted on the cramping literary conventions of the Scientific Paper (Medawar 1964; Bazerman 1988). An economist should be aware that he adopts more than a "mere style" when he adopts the conventions of a genre.

Pure theory in economics is similar to the literary genre of the marvellous (following here Tzvetan Todorov's distinction between the "marvellous," where the laws of nature are plainly violated, and "fantasy"—what would be called "horror fiction"—where the reader hesitates between realism and the marvellous, uncertain and afraid [1977 (1971), 156; 1973/75 (1970), chap. 2]). Like the marvellous the genre of economic theory violates the rules of "reality" for the convenience of the tale, and amazing results become commonplaces in a world of hypothesis. That animals exhibit the foibles of human beings is no surprise to a reader brought into a world in which animals talk. "Romance" is the older word. One of the earliest among modern literary theorists, Clara Reeves, gave in 1785 a definition of romance (quoted in Scholes and Kellogg 1966, 7) which would suit the latest production in the *Journal of Economic Theory*: "The Romance in lofty and elevated language, describes what never happened nor is likely to happen."

No blame attaches. The task of pure theory in economics is to invent marvels that have a point, the way *Animal Farm* has a point.

The plots and characters of pure theory have the same relation to truth as those in *Gulliver's Travels* or *Midsummer Night's Dream*. Pure theory confronts reality by disputing whether this or that assumption drives the result, and whether the assumption is realistic. Economists have long quarreled over the realism of this or that assumption. The literary analogy puts the debate in a strange light. It is the talking animals or the flying carpets that makes *The Arabian Nights* "unrealistic?"

Economists would do well to know what genre they are reading or writing, to avoid misclassifying the marvellous. Speaking of pure theory as marvellous, I repeat, does not put it at a low value. *Gulliver's Travels* is marvellous, too, but pointed, instructive, useful marvels for all that. Knowing the genre, though, is necessary for the critic and helpful for the artist. Economic and other theorists usually know what genre they are writing. They show it in their little jokes, of "turnpikes" along the way to economic growth and "bliss" points when you get there.

Yet the marvellous and romantic can be given too free a rein. Auden noted that "What makes it difficult for a poet not to tell lies is that, in poetry, all facts and all beliefs cease to be true or false and become interesting possibilities" (quoted in Ruthven 1979, 175). Some fields of economics consist mainly of interesting possibilities. The hundredth possible world of international trade theory gives the impression of an allegorical poesy gone whacko.

Good empirical work in economics, as already noted, is like realist fiction. Unlike fantasy, it claims to follow all the rules of the world. (Well . . . all the *important* ones.) But of course it too is fictional. The applied economist can be viewed as a realistic novelist or a realistic playwright, a Thomas Hardy or a Henrik Ibsen. The analogy on its face seems apt. Economics is a sort of social history. For all the brave talk about being the physicists of the social sciences, economists do their best work when looking backwards, the way a paleobiologist or geologist or historian does.

A certain kind of empirical work in economics, to continue the analogy, is like horror fiction, Todorov's "fantasy." Unlike the marvellous, it follows all the rules of the world except one, catching the reader unaware. Dr. Frankenstein is a wholly believable and ordinary figure except for his ability to make humanoids. A policy experiment may be wholly believable except for its introduction of a radical new policy, the reduction of the income tax form to a single page, say, or the elimination of securities regulation.

But wait a minute. To all this the modernist schoolmasters so long in charge of our intellectual life would reply crossly that it is my analysis that is the fantasy and fiction. The proper scientist *finds* the story. No fiction about it.

The answer to such an assertion has long been understood. The storyteller cloaks himself in Truth—which is what annoyed Plato about alleged imitations of life in sculpture or poetry. Just "telling the story as it happened" evades the responsibility to examine the point of view. Realist fiction does this habitually—which shows another use for the literary analogy, to note that realist fiction in science can also evade declaring a point of view. The sociologist Michael Mulkay notes in the epistolary arguments of biologists a Rule 11: "Use the personal format of a letter. . . . but withdraw from the text yourself as often as possible so that the other party continually finds himself engaged in an unequal dialogue with the experiments, data, observations and facts" (1985, 66). The evasion is similar in history: "the plot of a historical narrative is always an embarrassment and has to be presented as 'found' in the events rather than put there by narrative techniques" (White 1973, 20).

The suppression of the "I" in scientific writing is more significant than one might think. In the modern novel the suppression of the authorial "I" has resulted in a technique peculiar to literature, "represented speech and thought." Grammarians call it "unheralded indirect speech," the French *style indirect libre*. Any page or two of Jane Austen serves: "Sir Walter had taken a very good house in Camdenplace, a lofty, dignified situation, such as becomes a man of consequence" (1965 [1818], 107, Sir Walter's words ["dignified

. . . a man of consequence"] in Austen's mouth); "Could Anne wonder that her father and sister were happy? She might not wonder, but she must sigh that her father should feel no degradation in his change" (108; Anne's words ["sigh . . . no degradation"] in Austen's mouth).

The parallel technique in science might be called "represented Reality" or "unheralded assertion" or *style indirect inévitable.*" The scientist says: It is not I the scientist who make these assertions but reality itself (Nature's words in the scientist's mouth). Scientists pretend that Nature speaks directly, thereby effacing the evidence that they the scientists are responsible for the assertions. It's just there. The result is similar in fiction: "We [as readers] can not question the reliability of third-person narrators. . . . Any first-person narrative, on the other hand, may prove unreliable" (Martin 1986, 142). Thus Huck Finn, a narrator in the first person, misapprehends the Duke, and we the readers know he does. The scientist avoids being questioned for his reliability by disappearing into a third-person narrative of what really happened.

Yet, to say it once more, nothing is given to us by the world in story form already. The poet and critic J. V. Cunningham noted the limits of sheer observation: "it is not the direct observation of murders and of the process of detection that leads to the construction of a detective story. . . . What a writer finds in real life is to a large extent what his literary tradition enables him to see and to handle" (1976, 182). Or the critic Northrop Frye: "To bring anything really to life in literature we can't be lifelike: we have to be literature-like" (1964, 91).

We tell the stories just as we make the metaphors (and in truth, we decide on the logic and we construct the scientific facts, subject to the hints the world leaves in our path), as in the choice of continuity. John Keegan illustrates the general point in his military history, *The Face of Battle.* He speaks of the "rhetoric of battle history" (1978 [1976], 36) as demanding that one cavalry regiment be portrayed as "crashing" into another, a case of "shock" tactics. Yet an observant witness of such an encounter at Waterloo reported that "we fully expected to have seen a horrid crash—no such thing! Each [line of cavalry], as if by mutual consent, opened their files on coming near, and passed rapidly through each other" (149). Horses, it turns out, will not crash into each other, or into people, and so the usual story is falsified. A story is something told to one another by human beings according to human rhetorical conventions, not something existing ready-told in the very rocks or cavalry regiments or mute facts themselves.

Stories, in other words, are selective, the selection being done by their authors. In this they are similar to metaphors and models, which must select, too. We cannot portray anything literally completely, as Niels Bohr once illustrated to a class. He asked his students to *fully* describe a piece of chalk, to give every fact about it. The students found the task impossible. Description has to be radically selective. We cannot know the history of every atom in the chalk or the location of every atom that bears any relation to the atoms in the chalk. We decide what matters, for our purposes, not God's or Nature's.

The fictional writer selects like the scientist and invites the reader to fill in the blanks. Stories or articles can give only a sample of experience, because experience is overwhelmed with irrelevance: taking out the garbage, bumping the table, scratching the back of one's head, scanning the title of a book one was not looking for. What distinguishes the good storyteller or the good scientific thinker from the bad is a sense of pointedness. One damned thing after another is not a pointed story, or good science (cf. Bruner 1986).

The parsimony of scientific stories is not the result of some philosophy commending parsimony. It is a result of the way we read science, our ability to fill in the blanks, telling pointed stories in our culture. An economist can read the most unreadable and compressed production of a fellow economist if she participates in the same community of speech.

Wholly fictional stories are parsimonious in the same way. Skillful fiction, whether in the form of *Northanger Abbey* or *The*

Origin of Species, "stimulates us to supply what is not there," as Virginia Woolf remarked of Austen. "What she offers is, apparently, a trifle, yet is composed of something that expands in the reader's mind and endows with the most enduring form of life scenes which are outwardly trivial" (1953 [1925], 142). Remarking on her remark in turn, the critic Wolfgang Iser put it this way: "What is missing from the apparently trivial scenes, the gaps arising out of the dialogue—this is what stimulates the reader into filling the blanks with projections [the image is of the reader running a motion picture inside his head, which is of course why novels can still compete with television]. . . . The 'enduring form of life' which Virginia Woolf speaks of is not manifested on the printed page; it is a product arising out of the interaction between text and reader" (1980, 110–11).

As Arjo Klamer (1987a) has shown for the postulate of economic rationality, scientific persuasion, too, is like that. Persuasion of the most rigorous kind has blanks to be filled at every other step, whether it is about a difficult murder case, for example, or a difficult mathematical theorem. The same is true of those difficult pieces of recent economic history called economic policy. What is unsaid—but not unread—is more important to the text as perceived by the reader than what is there on the page. As Klamer puts it, "The student of the rhetoric of economics faces the challenge of speaking about the unspoken, filling in the 'missing text' in economic discourse" (175).

The running of different motion pictures in our heads is going to produce different texts as perceived. Todorov asks: "How do we explain this diversity [of literary readings]? By the fact that these accounts describe, not the universe of the book itself, but this universe as it is transformed by the psyche of each individual reader" (1980 [1975], 72). And elsewhere: "Only by subjecting the text to a particular type of reading do we construct, from our reading, an imaginary universe. Novels do not imitate reality; they create it" (67f.) Economic texts also are made in part by the reader. Obscure texts are often therefore influential. The crafty John Maynard

Keynes, for example, most influentially in *The General Theory of Employment, Interest and Money*, left many opportunities for readers to run their own internal motion pictures, filling in the blanks.

Well, so what? What is to be gained by thinking this way about economics? The big answer is the burden of the rest of the book: that by seeing their stories and metaphors together the economists and their audiences can resist the many charms of snake oil, and see that economists are wise, but not so smart. That is why an outsider to economic expertise might care that the experts kept their metaphors and stories lined up.

But consider one minor and internal answer: storytelling makes it clearer why economists disagree. Disagreement among scientists is suggestive for the rhetoric of science in the same way that simultaneous discovery is suggestive for its sociology.

The non-economist does not realize how much economists agree, back in the seminar room or the office. But he is not entirely wrong in thinking that they also disagree a good deal. Economists separate themselves into long-lasting schools, allegedly more typical of the humanities than the sciences (though any recent history of a science will give the lie to the journalistic assumption that science is agreement: such as Gould 1989, 19: "we [paleontologists] certainly do not agree about very much," a remark he documents in the rest of the book). A journalist will commonly end his television story about a new tax by complaining that the economists he has interviewed appear to disagree. He is not surprised that a story about a far-reaching change in economic policy evokes more disagreement than a story about a fire in the Holiday Inn. But if economics is a science, dammit, why can't economists agree?

One cause of disagreement is an oversimplified theory of reading. The theory of reading adopted officially by economists and other scientists is that scientific texts are transparent, a matter of "mere communication," "just style," simply "writing up" the "theoretical results" and "empirical findings." Communication is seen as the transmission of unaltered little messages through inter-mental pipes, in the manner of the hydraulic tube at the drive-in bank, or a sewer. The pipes occasionally get clogged up. That's a "communications problem." Then a Roto-Rooter of "let's be clear" reams out the pipes and lets the flow surge through.

If reading were so free from difficulties as this then naturally the only way our readers could fail to agree with us, after we have reamed out the pipes, would be on account of their dimness or their ill will. (Set aside the unlikely possibility that we the writers are the dim ones.) It's sitting right there in black and white. Don't be a dunce.

A better theory of reading sees scientific prose as being like liter-ary prose, complicated and allusive, drawing on a richer rhetoric than a narrow demonstration. The better theory is the one a good teacher uses with students. She knows well enough that the text is not transparent to the students, and she does not get angry when they misunderstand. God likewise does not get angry when his students misunderstand His text. In fact, like scientists and schol-ars, God writes difficult texts to ensnare us. St. Augustine, as the literary critic Gerald Bruns has noted, viewed the obscurity of the Bible as having "a pragmatic function in the art of winning over an alienated and even contemptuous audience" (1984, 157). The contrived obscurity is not nice but is not rare in science and re-ligion. Bruns quotes Augustine (who might as well be justifying the obscurities of a mathematical economist proving the obvious): "I do not doubt that this situation was provided by God to con-quer pride by work and to combat disdain in our minds, to which those things which are easily discovered seem frequently to be worthless" (157).

Even with a sophisticated theory of reading, though, the econo-mists would differ, because they come from different literary cultures. A scientist will come from a certain background, sup-plied with a language. Unless her reader knows roughly the same language—that is, unless he has been raised in approximately the same community as she has—he will misunderstand and will be unpersuaded. The misunderstanding is no more unforgivable than being non-French or non-Balinese. The reader comes from another culture, with a different tongue.

And even if the foreign culture is understood it may be rejected. A foolishly sentimental poem has the same irritating effect on a reader as does a foolishly libertarian piece of economics. The reader refuses to enter the author's imaginative world, or is unable to. A literary critic said, "A bad book, then, is a book in whose mock reader we discover a person we refuse to become, a mask we refuse to put on, a role we will not play" (Gibson 1980 [1950], 5). The reader therefore will of course misread the text, at least in the sense of violating the author's intentions. We do not submit to the authorial intentions of a badly done greeting card or of a scholarly argument written in a culture hostile to ours. In a well-written novel or a well-written scientific paper we agree to submit to the authorial intentions, so far as we can make them out. The entire game in a science such as biology or chemistry or economics is to evoke this submission by other scientists to authorial intentions. The general public submits in turn. The great chemist Linus Pauling for a long time commanded attention, and his readers submitted to his intentions, at least outside of vitamin C; the great economist Paul Samuelson likewise does so, at least outside of investment advice.

The argument can be pushed further. An economist expositing a result creates an "authorial audience" (an imagined group of readers who know this is fiction) and at the same time a "narrative audience" (an imagined group of readers who do not know it is fiction). As the critic Peter Rabinowitz explains (1980 [1968], 245), "the narrative audience of 'Goldilocks' believes in talking bears." The authorial audience realizes it is a fiction. The Roto-Rooter theory and the one-unified-culture theory cannot accommodate such an obvious point about real writing, that the authorial and narrative audiences (and authors) are different (compare Booth 1988, 105).

The difference between the two audiences created by the author seems less decisive in economic science than in explicit fiction, probably because we all know that bears do not talk but we do not all know that the notion of "marginal productivity" in economics is a metaphor. The narrative audience in science, as in "Goldilocks," is fooled by the fiction, which is as it should be. But in science the authorial audience is fooled, too (and so incidentally is part of the literal audience, the actual readers as against the ideal readers the author appears to want to have). Michael Mulkay, again, has shown how important is the inadvertent choice of authorial audience in the scholarly correspondence of biochemists. Biochemists, like other scientists and scholars, are largely unaware of their literary devices and become puzzled and angry when their literal audience refuses to believe in talking bears (1985, chap. 2). They think they are merely stating facts, not making audiences. Small wonder that scientists and scholars disagree, even when their rhetoric of "What the Facts Say" would appear to make disagreement impossible. Science requires more resources of the language than raw sense data and first-order predicate logic.

Taking economics as a kind of writing, then, explains some of the disagreements of economists and other academic folk. The explanation shows that the fact-logic half of the rhetorical tetrad does not suffice for human reasoning. Economists go on disagreeing after the "theoretical results and empirical findings" have been laid out for inspection not merely because they are differentiating their product or suffering from inflammation of the paradigm but because they read a story or a scientific paper written in an unfamiliar language ignorantly, yet do not recognize their ignorance. They are like the imperious British visitor to Florence who believes firmly that Italians really do understand English and can be made to admit it if one speaks slowly and loudly: WHERE . . . IS . . . YOUR . . . STORY??!

3   The Politics of Stories in
      Historical Economics

*I*f economists told stories about the economy they would be historians. Well, they do and are. They are not social engineers, though they want to be. They are social philosophers and above all social historians. Much of what they do is history in another key.

Stories of British Failure

An accessible and important instance is the story of British economic "failure" after 1870. The debate has flipped and flopped since the 1920s between prosecutions and defenses of the Victorians. The sons of Victorian fathers, prominent among them John Maynard Keynes, attributed Britain's difficulties between the wars to Victorians long dead. Around 1940 the charge was stated at length by historians such as Duncan Burn. During the early 1960s the case for the prosecution, thrice told, was brought to a peak of eloquence by historians such as David Landes. In the late 1960s and 1970s, unexpectedly, the Victorians acquired defenders, mainly Americans trained in technical economics, including myself. Around 1980 the prosecution was renewed by a new group of historians and historical economists, among them William Lazonick and Martin Wiener. And by the late 1980s the defense too had been renewed. The cycle of revision makes the head ache, but no more so than fifty other long-running economic controversies.

Because British history guides other histories the choice of metaphors and story lines in British economic history has more than academic interest. The continuity or discontinuity of the British

industrial revolution still shapes our ideologies. The British en-
closure movement of the eighteenth century is still viewed as a
model or anti-model for land reform. The British experience with
imperialism in the nineteenth century is still taken as typical. And
the British experience of being first in manufacturing and then dis-
gracefully "failing" is still supposed to contain a moral for us all.
Britain was the first industrial nation, and the first to become mature—some would say, with charming ageism, senile. Britain's
past looks to many like the world's future. We are all British in the
end. And if capitalism works, as others would claim, it should certainly have worked in Britain, most of all in the grand old days of
laissez faire, in that late Victorian age.

The economists Bernard Elbaum and William Lazonick, who
are dubious about the health of advanced capitalism and are
among the recent critics of Victorian businesspeople, favor medical metaphors of what went wrong. They speak of an "affliction,"
the "British disease," and "diagnosis" (Elbaum and Lazonick
1986, 1). The historians David Landes and Martin Wiener, who
argue that the culture of a mature economy favors leisure over
work, prefer the more bourgeois metaphor of a race (Landes
1969; Wiener 1981). Their metaphors of "leadership" in the
"race" appear for example in Landes's chapter headings, "Closing
the Gap" and "Short Breath and Second Wind"—and a military
version in "Some Reasons Why," taken from a poem about a cavalry charge.

The story is stated in a few pages of Landes's classic work of
1965, containing a conference paper of 1954, reprinted and extended as a book in 1969, *The Unbound Prometheus: Technological Change and Industrial Development in Western Europe from
1750 to the Present*. The main question of the middle third of
Landes's book is, "why did industrial *leadership* pass in the closing decades of the nineteenth century from Britain to Germany?"
(1969, 326, italics added). His answer is in brief: "Thus the Britain of the late nineteenth century basked complacently in the
sunset of economic hegemony. . . . Now it was the turn of the third

generation, the children of affluence, tired of the tedium of trade and flushed with the bucolic aspirations of the country gentleman. . . . They worked at play and played at work" (336).

Landes notes that the way the European story is usually told justifies the talk of footraces and cavalry charges among ironmasters and insurance brokers, and of the sunset of economic hegemony. The balance of power in Europe since Peter the Great is supposed to have depended on industrial leadership. Waterloo and the Somme are supposed to have been decided on the assembly line and trading floor. The supposed link between the lead in war and the lead in the economy became a commonplace of political talk before World War I and has never since left the historical literature. To think otherwise, says Landes, is "naive" (327).

The link, it needs to be pointed out, is doubtful. After all, a large enough alliance of straggling, winded followers could have fielded more divisions in 1914. The case again of Soviet Russia in 1942 or North Vietnam in 1968 suggests that military power does not necessarily follow from economic power. Landes is speaking a truth but an irrelevancy true by definition when he quotes a forward-thinking Frenchman of 1788: "The people that last will be able to keep its forges going will perforce be the master; for it alone will have arms" (326). The remark is literally true—no forge, no bayonet. But it is true by chemistry and definition, in the way that H_2O is 2 of H and 1 of O, with no substitution allowed. It is not true by economic fact and military history. In an economy there are substitutes for blood and iron, even if there are not in chemistry. The French in fact imported iron from their chief enemy throughout the Napoleonic Wars.

The literal extinction of forges has seldom caused defeat, notwithstanding the hardy myth that blockades and strategic bombing win wars (Olson 1963). The Union sacrificed more men than the entire United States did in any other war to put down a rebellion by a less populous section that it outproduced in 1860 by 30 to 1 in firearms, 24 to 1 in locomotives, and 13 to 1 in pig iron (McPherson 1988, 318). In World War I the shovel and barbed wire, hardly the most advanced fruits of industry, locked the Western Front. Strategic bombing, using the most advanced techniques and the most elaborate factories, failed in World War II, failed in Korea, and was therefore tried again with great fanfare, to fail again, in Vietnam. The equation of military power with economic power is good newspaper copy but poor history.

What is most wrong about the metaphor of leadership in a race of industrial might, though, is that it assumes silently that first place among the many nations is vastly to be preferred to second, or twelfth. Leadership is number-one-ship. In the motto of the great football coach, Vince Lombardi: "Winning isn't the most important thing, it's the only thing."

Landes reports correctly that "within fifteen years [of cheering the Prussian victory over perfidious France in 1870] . . . the British awoke to the fact that the Industrial Revolution and different rates of population growth had raised Germany to Continental hegemony and left France far behind" (1969, 327). He is correct that in fact the British in the 1880s did fret about German "hegemony" and did speak of the necessity to "awaken." The British at the time certainly did believe the Lombardi motto, *numero uno* or nothing.

It is the usual panic of the intellectuals, the sort we are seeing now in the United States vis-à-vis Japan and Europe. The journalists and professors are enchanted by the image of foreign trade as a football game. Yet historians do better to resist the sporting and military metaphors they find in their sources. Landes here yields to the magic, asserting unconsciously the importance of coming first *and only first*. For example: "To be sure, it is easy to demonstrate the exaggeration of these alarms. Germany's gains still left her far *behind* Britain as a commercial power. . . ." (328, italics added). Landes was not thinking critically about his historical sources or his economic story. The metaphors of disease, defeat, and decline are too harshly fixated on Number One to be right for an economic tale. The Lombardi motto governs narrowly defined games well enough. Only one team wins the Super Bowl.

The fixation of Number One, though, forgets that in economic affairs being Number Two, or even Number Twelve, is very good indeed.

The sporting metaphor, in other words, is not a good theme for the story of the British economy in the late nineteenth century. Its forty-five million souls were not trying to score points on Germany or the United States. They were trying to earn a living and gain the pearly gates, on their own, making individual choices daily with no collective goal in mind. In the century after 1870 the residence of the souls in Britain—or, better, in a world economy integrated from the mid-nineteenth century on—gave them steadily expanding choice; and they had been relatively rich at the outset. The prize for second in the race of economic growth was not poverty. The prize was great enrichment, if rather less enrichment than certain other groups of people, mainly poorer people. Since 1870, in other words, Britain has grown pretty damned well, from a high base.

By contrast, the diseases of which the pessimists speak so colorfully are romantically fatal; the sporting or military defeats are horribly total; the declines from former greatness irrevocably huge. An historian can tell the recent story of the first industrial nation as a failure, and be right by comparison with a few countries and a few decades. The historian would sell plenty of books to Americans in the last years of the twentieth century, because Americans—or at least the Americans who write the newspaper articles and frame the trade policies—are experiencing a new anxiety about "loss of leadership."

On a wider, longer view, however, the metaphor of failure in a race is strikingly inapt. Before the British the Dutch were the "failure." The Dutch Republic has been "declining" practically since its birth. With what result? Disaster? Poverty? A "collapse" of the economy? Not at all. The Netherlands has ended small and weak, stripped of its empire, no longer a strutting power in world politics, a tiny linguistic island in a corner of Europe—yet fabulously rich, with among the highest incomes in the world (now as in the eighteenth century), a domestic product per head quadrupling since 1900, astoundingly successful by any standard but Lombardi's.

Though inapt the pessimistic story is the dominant one. Failure to keep up in technological change, it is said, explains why British growth dropped after 1870, in comparison with its mid-century pace and in comparison with that of the new industrializing countries. The failure in turn is said to have caused British shares of world markets to fall. Martin Wiener's pessimistic storytelling, for instance, has Britain "surrendering a capacity for innovation and assertion" by 1901 (1981, 158). Such a remark jars in the alternative and optimistic story, which tells of a necessarily less bulky Britain engaging nonetheless in such innovation and assertion as radar, the Battle of Britain, jet engines, and the structure of deoxyribonucleic acid.

The way of telling stories, then, shape one's opinion about Victorian failure. The narrative circle—namely, that one needs the moral to tell the story, and yet the story makes the moral—is similar to the "hermeneutic circle" on the reader's side (that one needs to know the context to know the details, but the details to know the context). It is not breakable. The stories that Wiener or Landes or Lazonick or I want to tell about the Victorian economy will alter if not determine the stories we do tell, because on both sides the wished-for story will decide which of the infinity of facts are relevant. Elbaum and Lazonick want the story to be one of penalties incurred from an early start, as in a more sociological vein do Landes and Wiener. The story of the tortoise and the hare has lasting appeal.

The optimists like me want the story to be one of "normal" growth, in which "maturity" is reached earlier by Britain. The failures were by international standards small, say the optimists, even in the industries such as steel and chemicals in which Britain is supposed to have done especially badly. Everyone concedes that in shipbuilding, insurance, bicycles, and retailing, Britain did well. But whether it "did well" or not, its growth did not depend importantly on keeping right up with Number One. Britain in 1890 could have been expected to grow slower than the new industrial nations. The British part of the world got there first, and was therefore "overtaken" in rate of growth by others for a time. Belgium was another early industrial country and had a similar experience of relative decline, seldom noted. On the whole, with minor variations accounted for by minor national differences in attention to detail, the rich nations converge.

Nothing awful happens to Britain in this story, and no neurotic blame or xenophobic hysteria is in order. The falling British share of markets was no index of "failure," any more than a father would view his falling share of the poundage in the house relative to his growing children as a "failure." It was an index of maturity.

The main British story since the late nineteenth century is the more than trebling of British income as others achieved British standards of living or somewhat beyond. A 228 percent increase of production between 1900 and 1987 is more important than an 8 percent "failure" in the end to imitate German habits of attention to duty. Looked at from India, Britain is one of the developed nations. The tragedy of the century past is not the relatively minor jostling among the leaders in the front of industrial nations. It is the appalling distance between the leaders at the front and the followers at the rear.

The story can be told statistically, from the tables of the leading student of world growth and trade, Angus Maddison. He assembled recently the statistics of national output for thirty-one countries from 1900 to 1987. Expressed in the purchasing power of 1980, some of the countries are given in table 1.

To use the image of the racecourse, the whole field, followers as well as leaders, advanced notably—usually by factors of three or more since 1900 in real output per head. The main story is this general and surprising advance. The tripling and more of income per head relieved much misery and has given life-affording scope to many people otherwise submerged: think of your great-grandparents. Out of Maddison's thirty-one cases, Japan was a follower

Table 1   The Statistical Fate of Nations: Rich and Poor in 1900 and 1987
(in dollars of 1980 purchasing power)

Country	National Product per Head		Factor of Increase
	1990	1987	
Rich Countries			
United Kingdom	$2,798	$9,178	3.2
Belgium	2,126	8,769	4.1
France	1,600	9,475	5.9
Germany	1,558	9,964	6.4
United States	2,911	13,550	4.6
The Newly Rich			
Japan	677	9,756	14.4
The Enrichening			
South Korea	549	4,143	7.5
USSR	797	5,948	7.5
The Newly Poor			
Argentina	1,284	3,302	2.6
The Poor			
India	378	662	1.8
Mexico	649	2,667	4.1

Source: Angus Maddison (1989, 19).

that became a leader, Argentina a leader that became a follower. South Korea and Taiwan have exhibited such astonishing growth recently (output per head growing by a factor of eight since 1950) that they fit in a special class, on the Japanese model. Excluding these four cases the race has been run as shown in table 2.

It was not until around 1980 that the followers finally reached the post the leaders had passed eighty years before, for reasons that economists still do not adequately understand (except to understand that the lag is not a matter of imperialist extortion). It would seem that one quarter of the growth in the rich countries from 1900 to the present might be assigned to special advantages

Table 2   Product per Head has Increased Everywhere Since 1900, Though
More Among the Rich than the Poor

	1900	1987	Factor of Increase 1900 to 1987
Leader Countries (15)	$1,893	$10,235	5.4
Follower Countries (13)	573	2,270	4.0
Factor of Difference at One Date	3.3	4.5	

Source: Maddison (1989).
Note: Leaders: Australia, Austria, Belgium, Canada, Denmark, Finland, France, Germany, Italy, [setting aside Japan], Netherlands, Norway, Sweden, Switzerland, United Kingdom, United States. Followers: Bangladesh, China, India, Indonesia, Pakistan, Philippines, [excepting South Korea and Taiwan], Thailand, [excepting Argentina], Brazil, Chile, Colombia, Mexico, Peru, USSR.

the rich countries earned or acquired. But three quarters of their growth (which is 4 times $1,893 divided by the end-state of $10,235 per head in the rich countries) is attributable to worldwide forces, forces powerful enough to overcome even the obstacles to growth in the average poor country.

   In other words, the trouble with the pessimistic choice of story in the literature of British failure is that it describes the happy outcome of Britain's growth as a tragedy. Such talk is at best tasteless in a world of real tragedies—Argentina, for example, once rich, now subsidizing much and producing little; or India, trapped in poverty after much expert economic advice. At worst the pessimism about Britain is immoral self-involvement, nationalist guff accompanied by a military band playing "Land of Hope and Glory." The economists and historians appear to have mixed up the question of why Britain's income per head is now six times that of the Philippines and thirteen times that of India—many hundreds of percentage points of difference which powerful forces in sociology, politics, and culture must of course contribute to explaining—with the more delicate and much less important questions of why British income per head in 1987 was 3 percent less than the French or 5 percent more than the Belgian.

In the face of a world-girdling explosion of incomes the fixation on a trivial "lag" of Britain behind some of the other leaders demands itself a story. Probably the fixation arises from the pride of first place, à la Lombardi. Many in Britain bemoan the loss of Empire and delight in describing a powerful industrial nation of fifty-five million people as "a small island." The common man feels less important without an Empress of India at Buckingham Palace, and the intellectuals mope around the club regretting a lost vocation for instructing the natives. Many American leaders of opinion adopt the British despair and indulge in sage talk that "we must do better." Soon enough it will be stiff upper lips, old chaps, eh, what? In spoofing this lugubrious Anglo-Saxon attitude no one has improved upon Sellars and Yeatman, in their classic of sixty years ago, *1066 and All That*. Their précis of memorable English history from blue Celts and Boadicea to modern times ends abruptly on page 115, after the Great War—because then "America became Top Nation and history came to a. [full stop]"

Meta-stories

The conventions of storytelling have affected the literature of Victorian failure in another way. The stories have ideological significance. The meta-narratives of politics can remain tacit, as in Wiener's writing or my own, or can be declared openly. Elbaum and Lazonick are admirably open: "In historical perspective, however, state activism must be absolved from bearing primary responsibility for Britain's relatively poor economic performance" because, after all, the poor performance by their story dates far back into the age of laissez faire (1986, 11). They end their chapter by attacking the Thatcher government for its "supposition that there are forces latent in Britain's 'free market' economy that will return the nation to prosperity." They express confidence instead in "the economic benefits of industrial planning" (16).

And the story of the scholarly literature itself matters. To repeat: "Our lives are ceaselessly intertwined with narrative, with stories that we tell and hear told, . . . *all of which are reworked in that story of our own lives that we narrate to ourselves"* (Brooks 1985, 3). Control over the historiography is as important as control over the history itself. Economists and historians tell stories of their own scholarly lives and attempt to impose them on others (a brilliant recent development of the theme in technical economics is Weintraub 1991).

In the academic story about Victorian economic stories the ruling metaphor, as in other essentially contested areas of economics or history, has not been steady accumulation of knowledge but conflict. Elbaum and Lazonick begin their edited volume of 1986 with an account of the wicked neoclassical economists arrayed against the rest, and in particular against the brave Marxists. Thirteen years earlier McCloskey and Sandberg (1971) had done the same with a different set of heroes and villains. It is not hard to guess how the stories were framed in both cases: this essay, both said, is the culmination of the long struggle against Error.

The historical writer must place himself at the end of a story that makes dramatic sense. Thus another contributor to the debate over Victorian economic failure, Robert Allen, who follows McCloskey more closely than is profitable to say, devoted the opening pages of an otherwise technical article imitating McCloskey's work to an intellectual history putting distance between himself and McCloskey (Allen 1979). In mathematics such remarks are the motivation, the story of our own lives, how God led me, His prophet, into the light.

Since historians and economists are trained to be ignorant of their rhetoric they do not notice themselves making a story of their own lives. In particular they do not apply the same standards they would apply to the history itself. Economists are especially inept here, because they get no self-conscious training in the telling of plausible stories. Other scientists, believing themselves to be nonhistorical, share the ineptness. A chemist's understanding of even the recent history of chemistry will consist of whiggish just-so stories about true enlightenment dawning. It is not surprising to find that historical geologists and paleontologists and the historians themselves can read the history of their disciplines better. But even so the historians will apply lower standards to the history of the controversy than they apply to the subject. Suppression and mis-reporting of evidence about academic controversy prevails among scholars professionally devoted to stopping the suppression and misreporting of evidence.

Consider Martin Wiener's (1981) attack on the historical and optimistic economists. The intellectual history developed in the appendix to his book is steeply slanted, as is the custom in such histories. A famous footnote 11 in the appendix is a good example. Footnotes, as professors know, often contain the meta-stories. Wiener begins by citing (incorrectly) the economist William Kennedy's criticism of McCloskey's lucubrations, but none of McCloskey's various replies, some of them devastating to Kennedy's approach. He quotes the economic historian Peter Payne as having doubts in 1974 that Victorian businessmen did well, but does not quote his contribution to the volume of *The Cambridge Economic History of Europe* (1978, 208–10), where the doubts fade. He characterizes favorable reviews by Barry Supple of McCloskey's iron and steel book and by Berrick Saul of Floud's engineering book as "critical." He identifies the historical economist Douglass North, one of the founders, as a critic of historical economics, and therefore presumably an ally against the economists who found Victorian business to have performed well. And he concludes by citing the hostile comment on McCloskey's 1970 paper by the historical economist Nicholas Crafts (1979) without citing the harsh but effective reply McCloskey (1979) made in the pages following in the same issue. Wiener presents himself, in other words, as taking an unbiased selection of the writing on Victorian economic growth. His story is in fact notably biased, a selection from one half of the evidence. If Wiener used such techniques elsewhere in the book (he does not), no historian would believe him.

The point is not that Wiener is alone in sin. Let the person who has never invented an intellectual history in a family quarrel or a scholarly debate step forward now to cast the first stone. The point is that an ersatz story of the scholar's life in scholarship will not do.

The ersatz history depends often on vulgar sociology or on still more vulgar political determinism. Here, not irrelevantly, Wiener does win a special prize. For example, he "explains" the views of the eminent Marxist historian Eric Hobsbawm as a reflex of his Marxist "dogma" and McCloskey's views as dogma "from a very different ideological standpoint" (168, 169). Wiener's rhetorical turn here is called "motivism," the notion that if I claim to have established your motive for making a certain argument (established by low standards of persuasiveness) I have in some way undermined your argument (Booth 1974, 24ff.). Thus: "You are a Marxist, as readers of the *Times* will surely know, which is why you argue that the struggle for the control of the workplace was important in the nineteenth century. Aha! I've got you there!" As it happens, neither the central planners nor the free marketeers in the controversy about Victorian failure have recourse to this argument from origins, perhaps because they have been so often its victims. Only the middle of the spectrum views intellectual Mc-Carthyism as innocent fun.

Even plausible sounding sociologies of science often do not square with what the natives know. (Anthropologists nowadays are haunted by the worry that they are not getting the jokes about Samoan sex life or the headhunting of the Ilongot; see Rosaldo 1987, Geertz 1988.)

One story in the sociology of Victorian historiography, for example, would go something like this. David Landes, eminent historian at Berkeley and then at Harvard, ace squash player and collector of antique clocks, master of the French of Paris, is one of a line of anti-economic "institutionalists," dating from Sombart's German Historical School of the last century. Landes's work was first drafted in his youth for a conference in 1954, influenced by Arthur H. Cole at the Harvard Business School. In 1946 Cole had written: "the hypothesis—almost invariably taken as self-evident—that the aim of all businessmen is and always has been the maximization of profits has been a primary element in economic theory over many decades, but actually no one has collected evidence to establish the truth of this contention" (1953 [1946], 188). This is the gauntlet that the historical economists at length picked up. One of them, Alexander Gerschenkron, a Russian-Austrian-American economist of great erudition, destined to develop into one of the doyens of the field, was at the time at Harvard, a young professor of economics (though senior to Landes), across the Charles River from Cole (who was senior to Gerschenkron). Gerschenkron picked up the gauntlet in a dispute with Landes that during 1953 and 1954 crowded the pages of Cole's journal, *Explorations in Entrepreneurial History.*

(One of history's cunning passage is that *Explorations,* the institutionalist's journal, became eventually *Explorations in Economic History,* devoted largely to establishing by anti-institutionalist means that businesspeople did indeed maximize profits.)

Later, in 1966, Gerschenkron assigned McCloskey, his graduate student in economics, to discuss Landes's book in Landes's presence at a dinner seminar. An analysis of all this in the style of the Columbia sociologist Robert Merton would seem straightforward: Marshall/Gerschenkron/McCloskey and numbers against Sombart/Cole/Landes and words; neoclassical economics against institutionalist economics; professors assigning students to attack their opponents; lines of influence drawn like subway maps; one invisible college arrayed against another. History deceives with whispering ambitions / Guides us by vanities.

(Another of history's contrived corridors is that *Explorations in Entrepreneurial History* became under its new name the official journal of the Cliometric Society, of which McCloskey was a co-founder. Another is that Landes holds now a position in the very Department of Economics from which Gerschenkron so long scowled at him.)

But that is not it at all. The sociology does not capture the correct story of the story. In fact Landes was willingly open to criticism at the dinner in 1966, as in 1970 at the first conference on the subject; and he was willing to play by the rules of the quantitative game (at which, unlike squash, he regularly lost). Gerschenkron was no fanatic against literary sources and was not in the habit of assigning students to attack his intellectual opponents. The term paper on the British iron industry from 1870 to 1913 that led to McCloskey's thesis and asserted its basic point was in fact written six months before he had heard of David Landes and his works, in the late spring of 1965. It was written for a course with Albert Imlah, a professor at Tufts University, no enemy of business or entrepreneurial history, who taught for Gerschenkron when the latter was on sick leave. McCloskey had not met Gerschenkron, had not decided to specialize in economic history, and did not know that Gerschenkron was skeptical of the entrepreneurial approach. *The Cambridge Economic History of Europe* was not published until 1965, and McCloskey did not read it until the dinner seminar (I have his earliest reading notes from January 1966). The word "entrepreneurship" was brought into the discussion of the British iron and steel industry not by Landes in 1965 (or 1954), but by Burnham and Hoskins in 1943 (271).

The only piece of true sociology in the situation looks a lot like rhetoric. When the question of economic performance arose, a young economist trained to speak like one in the late 1960s was likely to take up productivity measurement and the rhetoric of number; likewise, a young historian trained to speak like one in the early 1950s was likely to take up business history and the rhetoric of prose.

The point is that slapdash sociology, and especially a sociology of some narrowly construed interest, whether political or personal, does not make for good intellectual history. Intellectual history, I have said, is a rhetorical move in historical controversy. Vulgar Marxism or vulgar capitalism makes for bad stories in economic history; vulgar sociology makes for bad stories in the corresponding intellectual histories. Sophisticated sociology, yes, of course (for it amounts to rhetorical scrutiny); vulgar sociology, attributing thoughts to residence in Chicago or registration as a Democrat, no.

The literary critic Northrop Frye has written that literature "has somewhat the same relation to the studies built out of words, history, philosophy, the social sciences, law, and theology, that mathematics has to the physical sciences. . . . Pure mathematics enters into and gives form to the physical sciences, and . . . the myths and images of literature also enter into and give form to all the structures we build out of words" (1964, 127). Frye's stripping away of mathematics from the human sciences is two-culture talk and unnecessary. Economics is a human science and yet properly mathematical. But he is right about the other leg of the argument. Stories in economics take much from literature, broadly conceived, choosing continuity or discontinuity, delighting in the ironies of the tortoise and the hare, ranging intellectual armies against one another, telling a story of our own lives that makes us heroes in the end. Economists and other experts are going to resist historical fact and historical argument, unwisely, until they recognize that they themselves are historians, tellers of stories, in their economics and in their lives.

4   Economic Rhetoric in Aid
of the Story Line

*E*conomic stories depend on rhetoric. The point is not to expose the rhetoric and then condemn it for being rhetoric. Rhetoric is unavoidable. An economist or historian cannot avoid writing rhetorically since any argument has a rhetoric, a style of argument, taking "argument" to mean "any designs on the reader." A collection of random facts and assorted bits of logic does not add up to an argument; but as soon as a writer advocates a model or a story in which the facts and logic are to fit he has begun to argue. If one is to argue in favor of this or that story there is no way of being non-rhetorical. "Just give me the facts" is itself a rhetoric, Sergeant Friday arguing his case by claiming not to. Writing rhetorically is no more a crime than breathing rhythmically.

Matters of form, usually viewed as ornament, are commonly in fact matters of argument. Even in poetry, Paul Fussell notes, "The meter conducts the argument. The meter is the poem. The art of poetry is the art of knowing language and people equally well. It is an art whose focus is in two directions. . . . The knowledge of the way the reader will react when a technical something is done to him is what controls the poet's manipulation of his technique. To do something to the reader is the end of poetry" (1979, 104).

In explicitly historical work, of course, such as that on Victorian failure, much of the technical rhetoric is directed at the story, which carries much of the argument.

56

Ethos

Consider the first principle of rhetoric, that the presumed character of the writer affects how the words are read by an audience. The Greek word is *ethos,* which is to say, "habit," "character," "moral impression." Economic and historical writers lard their prose with ethical appeals. That is no surprise or scandal. We pay more attention to the President than to a congressional aide, more attention to the boss than to the assistant. A writer will of course present himself as worthy of scientific attention. Non-economists make ethical appeals in historical writing to the character of The Sophisticated Professional or The Historian. Everyone makes an appeal to ethos, if only an ethos of choosing never to stoop to such matters as ethos.

Some of the complexity in economics and therefore in historical economics amounts to the appeal, usually a risible one, to the ethos of The Scientist. Complicated machinery of intellect, *Dasein* or demography, fascinates everyone. Unhappily, obscurity in argument pays. A book by a French historian famous for his profound obscurity was recently translated into plain English. When thus made clear it turned out that his argument was simple, even a little simple-minded. The historian in his eminence was outraged by the lucidity of the translation. It did not capture, he complained, *"ma profondité."*

An appeal to the character of The Profound Thinker is sweet indeed. The education of an economist drills into him the ethos of The Scientist Dealing With Super Profound Matters. The historical economist William Kennedy, for example, has argued in profound terms that in Victorian Britain engineering and other progressive sectors should have grown faster: "the conservatively estimated gains from such counterfactual sectoral shifts of economic activity . . . [are] on the order of 25 percent to 50 percent of British GNP in 1913" (1982, 105). Shuffling around could have increased the output of the British economy by a quarter to a half. That seems remarkable.

The remarkable conclusion comes from a profound calculation: "The aggregate average rate of growth may be defined as a weighted sum of the average rates of the component sectors of the economy [equations follow defining the rate of growth of a whole as the growth rate of its parts]. . . . It is possible to transform the accounting identity defined in equation (1) to allow ready consideration of counterfactual possibilities as follows" (equations follow showing what happens to the growth of the whole when the growth of one sector rises). He then calculates the "counterfactual" with much effort in four large tables to five digits of accuracy.

Kennedy's argument assumes its conclusion, more directly than is usual even in economics. The argument begins and ends this way: If certain production had grown faster *without other production growing slower,* then British production would have been larger. Startlingly, that is all the difficult-sounding machinery of "may be defined" and "transforming identities" and "counterfactual possibilities" amounts to. The economics is literally that if 2 + 3 = 5, then 5 will grow if 2 does. The economic idea of scarcity—that a growing 2 might have to take some labor or machinery from 3—does not appear in his economics. If a professor wrote more books *and did not teach fewer hours* his combined output would be larger. If you watched more television *and did not spend less time at other activities* your day would be longer.

The argument is a "counterfactual" in a somewhat special sense. It does not ask what might reasonably have happened if our world had been modified in small ways; it contemplates a world of free lunches, in which British engineering could grow faster without other sectors having to pay. If more production could come from nothing, then Britain could have been richer. Well, yes. But if 25 or 50 percent richer, why not 100 or 500 percent, or 10,000 percent? All we need to do is to imagine a "counterfactual possibility" (engineering growing at 300 percent a year, say) and then confuse ourselves and others impressed with *profondité* by putting the number into a sum of many terms transformed by arithmetic.

Complicated arguments have this danger, that the complexity will conceal violations of good sense even from the framers. The point is a commonplace in scientific argument: "Mr. Brown's argument is so complex that it must be mere sand-in-the-eyes." Among economists for example the point has killed the large-scale statistical model, at least for scientific as against policy-making purposes. If one constructs a 500-equation model that cannot be reduced to simpler terms then one cannot hold any of its reasonings in mind. It ceases to be humanly persuasive. True, one can say, "Believe me: the model just works." The appeal persuaded economists twenty years ago. It no longer does (except again for certain tasks of prediction for policy). No one doubts a calculation on how to fly a spacecraft to Mars, despite its complexity, because we have great confidence in the law of gravity inside the calculations (though in fact perturbation theory in celestial mechanics has doubt-provoking complexities). But everyone doubts a blindingly complex calculation when the laws of motion are less well understood, as in economics.

Complexity has therefore also been used in the literature on Britain as the opposite of an authoritative ethos, as evidence of disauthority. This is the rhetorical plan in an essay by the historical economist Stephen Nicholas in 1982. Nicholas doubted the calculations of productivity made in the decade before that had restored Victorian businessmen to their reputation for competence. By the mere statement of the "assumptions" said to underlie the neoclassical calculation by the earlier economists he raises doubts in the minds of historians and economists. After a survey of the debate from Landes to 1982 in lucid prose, he starts off to "explain" the calculations to be criticized (86): "it is assumed [note the features of style borrowed from the language of mathematics] that the economic unit is a profit maximizer, subject to a linear homogeneous production function and operating in perfectly competitive product and factor markets. Given these limiting assumptions, the marginal productivity theory of distribution equates marginal products of factor rewards. It follows by Euler's theorem . . ." etc., etc.

To most of his readers in the *Economic History Review* he might as well have written "it is assumed that the *blub-blub* is a *blub* maximizer, *blub-blub blub-blub-blub* and *blub* in perfectly *blub* and *blub blub*. Given these limiting assumptions, the *blub blub blub blub blub blub*. It follows by *blub blub*. . . ." The audience that can understand the argument is the audience that already understands it. The people who do not understand it, who are most readers, get only the idea that "limiting assumptions" are involved (Nicholas makes a similar move in 1985, 577). The passage takes the outward form of an explanation. But the explanation merely terrifies the onlookers, as it intends to, convincing them that the neoclassical calculation makes a lot of strange and unconvincing assumptions. (Though not to the point here, it happens that the calculation does not make any of the assumptions he mentions; it is a measure; it makes no more assumptions than a bathroom scale.) Nicholas is taking on the ethos of the Profound Thinker defending the innocents from other Profound (But Irresponsible) Thinkers.

Pathos

Parallel to ethos, the audience's attention to the speaker, is *pathos,* the speaker's attention to the audience, the effort to make the audience weep and cheer. Pathos shapes the implied reader. Consider again Landes's essay of the 1960s, so plainly "using rhetoric" (though bear in mind that "using rhetoric" is not confined to the best writers, such as Landes; rhetoric is not merely elegance). The implied reader of Landes's essay is made into an ally. The reader is part of the "our" in "It is now time to pull the threads of *our* story together and ask *our*selves why the different nations of western Europe grew and changed as they did" (1969, 326; italics added). Landes sidles up to the reader. The particular appeal to pathos by the historian Landes contrasts sharply to that by the historical economists, such as Robert Fogel or Donald McCloskey, with their vulgar and lawyerly ways. The implied reader of these Perry Masons is either an imbecile who holds the views Fogel or Mc-Closkey are demolishing or else an enthusiastic ally joining them in sneering at the imbecile. Controversy in mathematics and in history is more often muted, even when its style is sharp and bright. Only a rare historian, such as J. H. Hexter, will shape the audience in the same aggressive way as do the historical economists, such as early Fogel or McCloskey. Landes's implied reader is made sweeter.

Style

Then style. A rhetoric of stories will watch the words closely. Watch, for instance, this: a text attempting to be authoritative uses the gnomic present, as in the sentence you are reading now, or in the English translation of the Bible, or repeatedly, again, in David Landes. Landes makes it a substitute for explicit social scientific theory, a function it serves in applied sociology and in much of the economic literature on growth, too. Thus in one paragraph on page 335 (italics added): "large-scale, mechanized manufacture *requires* not only machines and buildings . . . but . . . social capital. . . . These *are* costly, because the investment required *is* lumpy. . . . The return on such investment *is* often long deferred." The last two sentences of the paragraph, by contrast, revert to the ordinary narrative past: "the burden *has tended* to grow . . . *has become* a myth."

The gnomic present claims the authority of General Truth (which is another of its names in grammar). But it sidesteps whether the truth asserted is a historical fact (that in actual fact the return on "such investment" in 1900 was by some relevant standard long deferred) or a timeless scientific metaphor (that in economics of the sort we are talking about most such returns will be long deferred), or perhaps merely a logical tautology (that the very meaning of "social capital" is taken to be investment of a generally useful sort with long-deferred returns). The one meaning in the tetrad borrows prestige and persuasiveness from the other. The usage says: "I speak as a historian, telling you historical facts about Europe, this being one; but I am also a social scientist in command of the best modeling, of which I am giving you a fine example; and if you don't like that, consider that anyway my truth is logically true by definition."

The gnomic present bulks large in Landes's argument, which is again no scandal. Landes uses the device as a substitute for economic theory. He needs some device for economic storytelling, and the device of the gnomic present holds the story together as well as would explicit economic theory. Note the tense at page 336, for example, after some *aporia* (rhetorical doubt) concerning whether it is true or not, "Where, then, the gap between leader and follower *is* not too large to begin with . . . the advantage *lies* with the latecomer. And this *is* the more so because the effort of catching up *calls* forth entrepreneurial . . . responses." (italics added). That in general and as an economic law the advantage lies with the latecomer is offered as a deductive conclusion (no regular economic theory says so, but the gnomic present does). And in truth the conclusion does follow deductively from the earlier assertions, themselves expressed in the gnomic present (for instance, page 335, "There *are* thus two kinds of related costs."; italics added).

Statistics, too, contribute to a style supporting a story. The economists and the quantitative historians use a statistic as Proof, the appeals court in storytelling, just the facts, Ma'am. Landes and other non-economists tend by contrast to use the statistics essay-style, the way quotations are used. Frequent as the statistics are by the standards of other sorts of history, in Landes' writing they nonetheless do not carry much of the argument. This may be seen in the casual way that he accounts for them, drawing freely on such questionable sources as *Mulhall's Dictionary of Statistics* (4th ed., 1909), a book of impossible wonders in fact making.

By contrast, in the writing of most historical economists the statistics are deployed monographically, the thing to be established, the output of the argument, the way the story is told, as in my use of Maddison's statistics in the last chapter. The economist Lars

Sandberg did the accounting of ring spinning in the Victorian cotton industry (1974, chaps. 2 and 3); the economists Peter Lindert and Keith Trace did the accounting of the Solvay process in the Victorian chemical industry (1971); the economist Charles K. Harley did the accounting of early industrial growth (1982). Whether they did them right is not the point here. The point is that economists favor the figure of argument making-a-set-of-accounts. Accounting is in fact the master metaphor of economics, the source of most of its quantitative bite. The metaphor alarms non-economists, puzzled by the cavalier way in which bits of number from disparate sources are flung into the calculation.

Poetics: Metaphor in Aid of Stories

A weighty matter of rhetoric is the choice of metaphors with which to tell the story: by what allegory will the narrator shape the data? In the hardest as in the softest science the choice of a metaphor reflects a worldview and the evidence to be examined. Worldview succeeds worldview. The metaphor is the message. As Stephen Jay Gould recently put it in connection with the triumph of time's arrow over time's cycle in geological theory, "Hutton and Lyell . . . were motivated as much (or more) by . . . a vision about time, as by superior knowledge of the rocks in the fields. . . . Their visions stand prior—logically, psychologically, and in the ontogeny of their thoughts—to their attempts at empirical support"(1987, Preface).

The sources of the metaphors applied to Victorian failure are various. Physiocracy among non-economists (and in the British Labour Party) takes industrial production of physical things as a part standing for the whole of output, excluding especially the much despised production of services (or "the 'production' of services," as Martin Wiener says with sneering quotation marks (1981, 157). If Victorians did better selling insurance than selling steel, as they did, the insurance is reckoned a nullity. Similarly the new "McJobs" in American service industries, such as nursing and education, are reckoned as not being real jobs, like mining coal or spinning cotton.

The verbal accounting changes the history. The distinction popular among historians and other non-economists between quantity and quality of life, to give another instance, will leave the economist cold. Income captures it all. In the economist's accounting the time to smell the roses makes people happy and costs something in opportunities forgone and is therefore also income. If British (and Japanese and German) people worked less intensely than Americans in 1900, as Gregory Clark has shown (1984), then the British (and Japanese and Germans) consumed a commodity called leisure in greater amounts than Americans did. Clark worries that social pressure on the job to take advantage of every chance to loaf may have cost more in income than the average British worker was actually willing to pay. But anyway the Americans bought their larger product with greater effort.

Having admitted to using metaphors the scientist asks then about their aptness or rightness. The anti-rhetorical frame of mind will want instead to speak of their truth or accuracy, words which apply to metaphors only metaphorically if at all. Well, says the modernist, it's a matter of positive Fact, is it not? What's the *accurate* metaphor of British growth and decline? The philosopher Nelson Goodman answers in the following way. "For nonverbal versions [of the world, such as a picture of British defeat in economic battle] and even for verbal versions without statements, truth is irrelevant. . . . The same considerations count for pictures as for the concepts or predicates of a theory: their relevance and their revelations, their force and their fit—in sum their *rightness*" (1978, 19).

A metaphor used in an economic story is not "true" in a simple way. "France is hexagonical" is neither true nor false in the way a statement in arithmetic is true or false (Austin 1975 [1962], 143–45). It is right, in a certain way of speaking, which is to say, useful for some purpose (though come to think of it one could say the same thing about statements in arithmetic). The methodology of Science that economists and other scientists believe they use gives no way to evaluate the rightness of metaphors. The assertion of likeness, so important in biology and physics, involves standards of likeness that can only be human and cultural. How similar *is* the smooth pea to the wrinkled, the planetary orbit to an ellipse, Latin 101 to a hog pen? These are questions about our use of language, constrained by the universe sitting out there, to be sure, but matters of human decisions about human usefulness.

Not seeing one's own human metaphors in storytelling while sneering at those of others is funny, as in the more adolescent flourishes of the new historical economists. One of them began a paper in 1970 concerning "Britain's Loss from Foreign Industrialization" with a sneer at the very idea of metaphor: "It is pardonable to use an occasional metaphorical flourish to elevate the commonplaces and simplify the complexities of economic history. The danger, however, is that the flourish will become an obstruction rather than an aid to thought" (141). The notion is that metaphors are merely ornamental, or perhaps merely aids to the slow-witted. The author proceeds to other pieces of literary self-consciousness: "The difficulty is that these metaphors [namely, those used by the less technically up-to-date Duncan Burn, Phyllis Deane, and W. A. Cole] have attached to them no clear literal meaning, or at best none that does justice to their connotations" (141). And so forth throughout. It does not occur to him that all language—and certainly the elaborate language of supply and demand "curves" that he then deploys with much claiming of Scientific ethos is irreducibly metaphorical. He later curls his lip in a dependent clause at the very idea, "*if* we must use metaphors" (McCloskey 1970, 152). Yes, my lad, we must. The critic and writer C. S. Lewis, followed by others, observed long ago that "the meaning in any given composition is in inverse ratio to the author's belief in his own literalness" (1962 [1939], 27).

Yet some metaphors are better, as we have seen. The students of metaphor are not saying that any version does as good a job as any other. The goodness of a metaphor, though, is not its merely propositional truth (whatever that might mean) but its aptness or rightness. Walt Rostow's famous metaphor of a "take-off" into self-sustained economic growth or Paul Samuelson's of consumers as calculating machines succeed or fail as ways of talking, our ways. The metaphor of leadership in economic growth, as was argued, fails because it veers off the subject, which is how well the economies do for their citizens, and directs attention to national vanity. The metaphor of winning replaces the metaphor of running well.

Inventio

Rhetoric concerns *inventio*, too, the finding of arguments. Rhetoric does not concern what one personally likes, in the way one likes chocolate ice cream. It concerns which arguments one is compelled by the conversation to take seriously. In the present case the main instance is: assessing British failure depends on taking comparison seriously. The assumption of failure involves comparisons left unmade. One cannot decide whether the British experience favors or disfavors capitalism by staring fixedly at Britain.

Historians such as Wiener (1981, 6–7) and Landes and economists such as McCloskey and Lazonick recognize the need to argue by comparison. If someone says that Britain failed compared to other countries he must have particular comparisons in mind. Landes and Wiener look to the German Empire; McCloskey and Lazonick to the United States.

Elbaum and Lazonick are only the latest Americans to emphasize that a notion of comparative failure must rest on comparisons across countries (1986, 2). Ironically, Elbaum and Lazonick themselves have been caught in their own failure to compare, by Gary Saxonhouse and Gavin Wright (1984, 1987; see Lazonick 1987; Elbaum and Lazonick 1986 does not mention the critics). Britain's "inflexible nineteenth century institutional legacy of atomistic economic organization" (Elbaum and Lazonick 1986, 15; compare p. 2) seems to have been as characteristic of Japanese cotton textiles as of British. But the Japanese cotton textile industry was flexible enough to seize the world market after 1918. Something has gone wrong with the notion that "atomistic economic organization" is to blame for British failure. What has gone wrong is ignoring the relevant device of rhetorical invention: comparison.

Historians focused on Britain itself are liable to miss the rhetorical point, gathering elaborate evidence of failure that is not comparative and therefore unpersuasive. A paper by Donald Coleman and Christine MacLeod (1986) provides an instance of the historical side. They collect evidence about British events without looking outwards. Stephen Nicholas provides an instance on the economic side. Nicholas recalculates productivity by allowing for his guesses about monopoly and economics of scale, and finds the amended productivity growth small in Britain from 1870 to 1914 (1985, 580). Unfortunately it does not occur to him that the point is necessarily comparative, and so he does not then subject the American or German statistics to similar tortures. The mistake is embarrassing because America and Germany were growing much faster. The allowance for their economies of scale would therefore turn back to spoil his argument about Britain.

The historian will say, "Though I have not compared, I have collected facts." The master metaphor in history—surprisingly unimportant in economics—is A True Account of Events, Based on Primary Sources. The metaphor of "collecting facts from the archives" tends to crowd out more apt and more rhetorical descriptions of the historian's business (Megill and McCloskey 1987). No historian who has faced the archival opulence of the nineteenth century can claim that he writes down everything he finds in the archives. Similarly, no economist who has faced the theoretical opulence of twentieth century economics can claim that he merely follows the logic he finds on the blackboard. If the Facts and Logic were enough to settle the matter with ease then it would long since have been settled. That is to say, if the facts and logic were as simple to state and to interpret as the rhetoric of the disputants suggests, then only malice and passion could explain why the others do not agree with Me or Thee (and sometimes I wonder about Thee).

We cannot leave it at that. To do so leaves the question to be settled by irrelevancies—by one's political fancies, chiefly, un-argued in the style of a preference for chocolate ice cream; and personal favor when politics provides no guide. Half the rhetorical tetrad is not enough. In the debate on Victorian failure the levels of asserted "fact" from most global to most individual are:

Capitalism is terrible.

Britain failed in the age of capitalism.

British ironmasters failed from 1870 to 1914.

Profitable opportunities X, Y, and Z in iron were ignored.

Such-and-such a measure of profit in X, Y, and Z is less than another.

British businessmen had thus-and-such mental or emotional deficiencies.

None strictly implies the other. Yet they are properly connected in rhetoric, it being more plausible that entrepreneurs in iron and steel failed if they appear to have ignored profitable opportunities. The rhetoric needs to be made explicit.

Consider for example the rhetoric surrounding the proposition at the fourth level down, that profitable opportunities were ig-nored. The optimists wish to connect it with the next lower proposition, that such-and-such a profit falls short of some other. The main criticisms of this optimist move have been that (1) it "uses neoclassical theory" (Coleman and MacLeod 1986, 598; Nicholas 1982, 85), and (2) that the measures refer to the "short run."

Neither is correct. The history here has gotten tangled up in a battle about the status of economic theory. The black beast of neo-classical theory is actually a small and closed set of mathematical economists. They do indeed "assume" strange behavior and then proceed to strange conclusions. But working economists do not "assume" all manner of perfection in people and markets, the "possession of the requisite information on costs and markets, knowledge of the available techniques" (as Coleman and Mac-Leod put it, 598). The factual inquiry aims precisely to test how good this or that "assumption" is (cf. McCloskey 1973, chaps. 1 and 2). To understand what the historical economists are doing one must abandon the Euclidean image of axiom and proof. Serious economists do not assume a can opener. They feel around in the historical drawer until they find it.

To mention a couple of cases important in Victorian Britain, the calculations of the profitability of East Midlands iron ore, say, and of the Solvay process in chemicals are merely second guesses. That is, the historian, not the historical actor, brings the "requisite information on cost and markets" to the calculation. The calculation sees whether or not the businessmen in question knew roughly what they were doing. The so-called neoclassical assumption in the simplest calculation says merely that businessmen wish to pay no more than what a thing is worth and are forced by competition to pay no less, within rough bounds. And more commonly the economists do not assume it even in this innocuous form; they test it.

If from the second guessing the businessmen prove to have been reasonably sensible in their choices then one concludes—not assumes—that they knew what they were doing (or else that they did not know what they were doing but were lucky, which appears to have been the case of American mechanical engineers in the nineteenth century: their traditions of hard driving suited the accidents of technical development). The calculation emphatically does not assume that they knew what they were doing—to make such an assumption would hardly be productive, since it is the question at issue.

The rhetoric of economics and of history, in short, goes beyond mere "style" in the ornamental sense of the word favored since the seventeenth century. It embodies how historians and economists argue. Calling the choices of metaphor, story line, and the like "mere style" is like calling the mathematics in physics or economics "mere formalism." Usually it is not. It makes the argument, which is all we have down here below the circle of the moon.

5 The Scholar's Story

*A*n example of economic storytelling is the work of Alexander Gerschenkron (1904–76), an unusual economist and historian exhibiting the tension between the two ways of telling stories. Born in Russia, educated in Austria, for long a professor of economics at Harvard, Distinguished Fellow of the American Economic Association and honored by his peers in other ways, he combined the humanistic learning of the German-speaking *Gymnasium* with the quantitative enthusiasms of American social science in the 1950s. He wrote on the mathematical theory of index numbers and on the literary theory of translation; with equal passion he read Greek poetry and listened to the Boston Celtics.

A person's life is an argument, though often unintended—we think less of Marx for his neglect of Jenny and his ignorance of physical work; and we think less of the modernist heroes of economics now for their frank appeals to selfishness, exhibited in their lives. Gerschenkron shaped much of his life to better values. Although addicted to a sly and not always amusing gamesmanship in his dealings with students and colleagues, he stood the bigger tests. In the year of tested values, 1968, for example, this private man spoke publicly against nihilism at Harvard, and when later the Soviet tanks rolled into Prague he spoke against international participation in a conference at Leningrad. Neither cause was successful: Harvard acceded to nihilism and the International Economic History Association met in Leningrad. Yet Gerschenkron persisted in persuasion.

His main scientific contribution was a "theory of relative back-wardness" (collected in Gerschenkron 1962d), which gave an account of the differing ways that European countries industrial-ized. He argued that a country like Russia, backward relative to Britain when it embarked on industrialization, did not go through the same stages. It leapt over them, using the centralized state as a substitute for the missing prerequisites of economic growth. Growth was force-fed in Russia, and to a lesser extent in Germany, with consequences for the character of the places. Russia grew with giant enterprises instead of small firms, centralized control instead of competitive markets, an overbearing military-industrial complex instead of peace-loving capitalists.

The first point in a rhetorical criticism of the story is that Gerschenkron attempts, like any scholar, to make us look at the story through a particular grid. We cannot look at Gerschenkron's theory innocently, as a thing in itself. We place a grid over it, our own or his, measuring it along the lattices of the grid.

The usual grid is a folk philosophy of science. Historians and especially economists share a grid framed by modernism, with its forlorn ambition to predict and control. Gerschenkron might be said in this lingo to have offered a "hypothesis," itself properly part of a "hypothetico-deductive system," which can be "falsified" by "empirical testing" against "observable implications."

His own words sometimes echoed these popular misunder-standings of scientific method, telling a modernist story of his scholarly career. Thus near the beginning of "Economic Back-wardness in Historical Perspective" (1952, at age 48 [reprinted in 1962d, 6, to which reference is made here], italics added): "histor-ical research consists essentially in application to *empirical material* of various *sets of empirically derived hypothetical gener-alizations* and in *testing the closeness of the resulting fit,* in the hope that in this way certain *uniformities,* certain typical situa-tions, and certain *typical relationships among individual factors* in these situations can be ascertained." And elsewhere he would say repeatedly that the concept of relative backwardness ("concept" and "process" were favorite placeholders in Gerschenkron's prose) is "an operationally usable concept" (1962c [1962d, 354]).

The words did not in Gerschenkron's practice carry the freight they usually do in economics. They did not impel him, for example, to throw away evidence on the grounds of alleged epistemological infirmity (he used both statistics and novels as sources for economic history; he used the absence of accounting terms in the Russian language of the eighteenth century to indicate the absence of commercial attitudes (1968, 449; 1970, 81). Though he detested the ruthless politics of the professorial chair that so shamed the scholarship of Europe, he did not pretend that he had no political arguments to make.

Above all, the vocabulary of social Science in the 1950s did not in the end ensnare Gerschenkron in social engineering. He rejected the notion that society was predictable. Social engineering requires prediction in detail. Gerschenkron looked to the past for wisdom, the delphic warnings that the past can give. He did not look to it for a blueprint of the future. Prediction and control, the promise of modernism, seemed to him narrow and impractical.

During the 1950s Gerschenkron outgrew a narrowing method, as many have. The great German classicist, Ulrich von Wilamowitz-Moellendorff, wrote of his own fascination with method:

Philology had [in 1870] the highest opinion of itself, because it taught method, and was the only perfect way of teaching it. Method, *via ac ratio,* was the watchword. It seemed the magic art, which opened all closed doors; it was all important, knowledge was a secondary consideration. . . . Gradually the unity of science [i.e. *Wissenschaft* = inquiry] has dawned on me. . . . Let each do what he can, . . . and not despise what he himself cannot do. (1930 [1928], 115)

The grid of folk philosophy and its Methods attributes a magic art to science.

The folk philosophy is not entirely useless. Its demarcations go some way towards classifying scholarship: scientific/non-scientific, objective/subjective, positive/normative, observable/non-observable, justification/discovery. But they do not go very far.

They cannot show science on the ground and at the bench, and they make a poor start at telling a scholar's story. An observer of science using them cannot see for instance why scientists disagree, since every scientist claims stoutly to operate on the good side of each demarcation—scientific, objective, positive, observable, and justificatory. The grid therefore worsens disagreements. It leaves the scientist to conclude that a disagreement must signal incompetence, some "unscientific" deviation in the opposition, which leaves him permanently angry at the incompetence of his colleagues. The grid of folk philosophy is itself unscientific, a bad description, and a bad moral theory of scholarship, with bad outcomes.

More often Gerschenkron himself invited the use of another grid, the practical philosophy of the scholar, an older scholarly ethic than the modernism of the mid-twentieth century. He held an elaborate and attractive theory of scholarship, exhibiting Continental values. The life's story represented in his work was that of The Scholar, an Immanuel Kant or a Jacob Grimm pondering over books by the late night's lamp. In a way that contrasts with British and some American traditions he practiced, as he affirmed often, "a program of research," less a method than a plan of life. His range as a scholar—at ease with mathematics, history, statistics, and a dozen languages—was subordinated to the program. The program was to yield not sharp or mechanical "tests of the theory," in modernist style, suitable to prediction and control, but mature judgments. The judgments would satisfy, as he frequently put it, "a sense of reasoned adequacy."

The phrase is not without mystery, but he did not intend the reasoning to be kept mysterious. The modernist asserts without looking at the history of science that only her method, *via ac ratio,* yields clear and distinct ideas. But the range of the *ratio* is too narrow, though clear and distinct within it. It resembles the method of the drunk who looks for his keys under the lamppost because the light is better there. The extreme explicitness of modernist reasoning under the lamppost is accompanied by extreme vagueness outside its range. Gerschenkron admitted all parts of the rhetorical tetrad.

Some matters of scholarship would need to remain tacit, but Gerschenkron had no patience with the unfootnoted *argumentum ex cathedra,* even from eminent scholars. Repeatedly he advocated and exhibited explicitness in argument. For instance, in his review in 1953 of Franco Venturi's *Il Populismo russo* (1968, 455), though congratulating Venturi for a "mature understanding," he complains that "one cannot but wish that the author had decided to share his thinking more fully with his readers." In a similar vein he warmly praised his student Albert Fishlow for "the statistical appendixes in which the author offers a full insight into his laboratory and without which no real appreciation of the importance of the study and of the validity of its interpretative results is possible" (1965, viii).

The scholarly ethos of care is prominently commended in Gerschenkron's reviews and in his footnote polemics. Carefulness in the European scholarly tradition has two parts, avoidance of error in detail and modesty in the putting forward of conclusions. We stop believing someone who makes little errors ("Bad spelling, bad reasoning") or who draws conclusions hastily ("How can he say such a thing?"). Gerschenkron here does not inhabit the world of modern economics, in which theory is said to provide a check on facts and in which a blackboard exercise is said to have "policy implications." Most particularly he detested theories of history that could in their rigidity supply bridges across evidential voids— Marxism most notably—and favored theories such as Arnold Toynbee's pattern of challenge and response that provided merely a way to shape the facts into a story. In this he was a modern professional historian, whose discipline is not economic or historical theory but the shaping of stories constrained by fact.

But neither the folk's philosophy of science nor the scholar's credo of virtue is much of a grid for measuring Gerschenkron. A better grid is rhetoric. A successful scholar and scientist above all engages in argument, and Gerschenkron lived a life of argument.

Gerschenkron's style of writing was the most obviously "rhe-

torical" support for his arguments. He delighted in obscure but
fine words, such as "flummox," a special favorite. He spoke mainly in the idiom of cultivated Europe, which made some sentences
in his earlier writings pure Latin. Most of the prose in his most
famous and earliest article on the subject, "Economic Backwardness in Historical Perspective," though lucid, is undistin-
guished. He appeared to be playing the sober scientist and waxed
eloquent only when the subject turned to ideology ("Ricardo is
not known to have inspired anyone to change 'God Save the King'
into 'God Save Industry' " [1952 (1962), 24f]).

Again, ethos figures heavily in Gerschenkron's rhetoric. He
wrote judgmentally about scholarly discourse, raising up or
breaking down the ethos of other scholars. Such judgments are
usually suppressed in scientific prose. In a few pages early in
Europe in the Russian Mirror he admired Tugan-Baranovskii
(1970, 6ff.: "valuable contribution"; "probably the most original
Russian economist, . . . amazingly broad in his interests"; and,
his greatest compliment, "a serious scholar"). Such compliments
serve more to honor the author than the subject—which after all is
their rhetorical purpose. The author exhibits the good taste to admire the best work. The old Russian economist's "amazingly
broad interests" turn out to be merely subjects within economics;
whereas the writer himself, also a Russian economist, ranged over
statistical theory, Western literature, and the history of baseball.

Waiting in Gerschenkron's office for an interview one day a
graduate student received from the nearest of numerous stacks of
books and magazines a lesson in the scholarly life, the sort of
lesson that professors forget they give. The stack contained a book
of plays in Greek, a book on non-Euclidean geometry, a book of
chess problems, numerous statistical tomes, journals of literature
and science, several historical works in various languages, and, at
the bottom of it all, two feet deep, a well-worn copy of *Mad*
magazine. Here was a scholar.

Beyond his style and ethos, Gerschenkron himself recognized the
rhetoric in science, and especially he recognized social theories as

metaphors. He was aware that words are not mere tags for things behind them but have their own force in the scholar's argument. His main contribution to scholarship was to revise radically the metaphor of social "stages," which had dominated nineteenth-century and much twentieth-century social thought. Henry Maine, Auguste Comte, Friedrich List, Karl Marx, Werner Sombart, Bruno Hildebrand, and latterly Walt Rostow thought of a nation as a person, with predictable stages of development from birth to maturity. The stage theorists took the child to be the father of the man; Gerschenkron was the new Freud, noting the pathologies arising from stages missed or badly taken, casting doubt on iron laws of succession.

He favored his own metaphors of "spurt" and "relative backwardness" as against "take-off" or "absolute prerequisites," but not because he believed his to be less metaphorical. Word-lore was no ornamental appendage to Gerschenkron's work: in the philological traditions of Europe the word was the work. He was aware in particular of the economistic character of his own metaphors, especially the notion of "substitutes" for prerequisites. "The German investment bank was a substitute for the missing or inadequate available prerequisite" (1970, 103). That is, in the illuminating jargon of neoclassical economics, the speed of industrialization arises from the "production function" with "substitutable inputs" of demand, finance, entrepreneurship, disciplined labor, and so forth. Scale has an effect, too: "along with differences in the vehemence of the process were the differences in its character" (72). The argument persuades economists in part because it relies on one of their master metaphors. At greater speed of industrialization certain inputs would rise in marginal product, as the economists say to themselves, and the Soviets would naturally build giant factories and crush a complaining peasantry.

Gerschenkron justified the economistic metaphor in a mainly Kantian rather than a Baconian way. He appears to have become in time more Kantian, becoming more convinced as Kant said that concepts without perceptions are empty, perceptions without concepts are blind. The classic essay on "Economic Backwardness" was first published in a volume edited by Bert Hoselitz in 1952. It is thoroughly British and Baconian. Things were as they were, open to common sense. The "story of European industrialization" (1952 [1962d, 26]) is a "story" only incidentally; really it is a scientific compound "synthesized from the available historical information" (7). There is no trace here of a story as a shaping fiction, disciplined by the facts of the matter but underdetermined by them. By 1962, however, at age 58, Gerschenkron is speaking in a different way. The "Postscript" to the first collection of essays, in 1962, speaks of "*viewing* European history as patterns of substitution" (1962d, 359; italics added). Failures of such a view "may be such as to require and perhaps suggest an *organizing principle* very different from the variations in the degree of backwardness" (364; italics added). And likewise in similar words.

The Kantian points of view are similar to weights in a statistical index of industrial output. That is, they are a choice, not things-in-themselves. Another distinguished economic historian much concerned with the scholar's life of words, William Parker of Yale, who was briefly a student of Gerschenkron's at Harvard in the early 1950s (most students were "briefly" his students: he supervised students in a somewhat casual way), has argued that Gerschenkron's experience of transplantation from Russia to Austria to America led him to the problem of point of view. Parker's story fits Gerschenkron's fascination with index numbers, relative backwardness, and literary translation (most notably a devastating assault on Nabokov's translation of Pushkin's *Eugene Onegin,* in *Modern Philology,* May 1966; see Gerschenkron 1968, 501–23).

Typologies are points of view. Gerschenkron warmed to the assigned task for "The Typology of Industrial Development as a Tool of Analysis," published first in 1962. He makes assertions about the uses of typologies that would be unintelligible to a natural Baconian, who believes that human typologies exist already in nature. To see the extremes of stages and of uniqueness in development as a unified pattern "does not at all mean that the extreme approaches are necessarily 'wrong' in any meaningful sense of the term. Since any approach of this kind . . . inevitably deals not with the unmanageable and incomprehensible 'totality' of the phenomena but with sets of abstractions, different approaches yield different insights, and it is in terms of those insights that the value of an individual approach must be judged. The results need not be commensurate" (1962b [1968], 79). And later: "Historical generalizations are not universal propositions that are falsified as soon as a single black swan has been observed. Our hypotheses are not 'lawlike' " (97).

Or consider the repeated images of "visualizing" in two pages of *Europe in the Russian Mirror,* published in 1970 (the very title and theme of the book, of course, mirrors the active vision; italics added): "Once we *view* the industrial development of Europe *in this fashion, it appears as* a unity. . . . Capital disposition is only one of very many examples of *an orderly pattern*" (103). Relative backwardness "gives us first of all *an opportunity to bring some order* into the apparent chaos, to *establish* [seeing actively is establishing] that is, a morphology or typology of the development" (104). Or elsewhere, on applying the typology to eighteenth-century mercantilism, "it *conceives* of Russia as a part of Europe" (87; and "regarded," "arrange," "picture," and "conceived" on the same page). Most Kantian of all, after quoting Goethe to the same effect, he writes: "What we call facts or reality, including Colbert or Napoleon, are just phenomena of a low degree of abstraction" (63). The scientist here is no passive observer of nature. He chooses his ways of worldmaking.

Facts passively observed constrain of course what can be seen, and Gerschenkron drew willingly on the rhetoric of British empiricism, too, if that is what the life of careful argument required. At the end of the passage just quoted he recurs to the nature of things (as against our way of seeing the things): "the degree of backwardness becomes then a causal principle, explaining for us the nature of the process of industrial change" (104). Even in this, however, he is pointing to the active observer, with the phrase "explaining *for us*." In the sentence leading up to the assertion of how things are (as distinct from how they seem) he insists on the shaping eye of the observer, who "sees" a "pattern," a morphology "temporarily seen." And the paragraph following returns to how we *see* the matter: "The more backward a country, the more barren *appears* its pre-industrial landscape. . . . This then is . . . my *picture* of European industrialization" (104; italics added).

Gerschenkron drew also on the doctrines of British empiricism to attack other theories, but again with Kantian supplementation. The trouble with stage theories, he says, is that "they are not very consistent with crude empiricism, and are damaged seriously when confronted with the relevant facts as we know them" (101). He appeals here to what "we," the scientific community, know; and the vocabulary of "consistent with . . . empiricism" and "confronted with the relevant facts," as fragments of modernist dogma. Yet he attaches "not very" to "consistent" and "crude" to "empiricism," distancing himself from a modernism that would forget Kant. Gerschenkron was of course an empirical worker, as any applied economist or historian must be, but a sophisticated one, who understood that scientists do not merely tally up the world's noumena.

Gerschenkron's theory, then, is by his own description "a way of looking" at the world. The metaphor of "substitution" is useful because it is "a construct that . . . helps to *conceive* Europe as a graduated unit" (108; italics added). Note that the virtue claimed is conversational. Talking this way will be helpful to the historical conversation. He speaks frequently of the theory as a classification or typology, by which he means the classification of botanical species (96), with Russia the red butterfly at one end and Britain the blue one at the other. He is hostile to mathematical or logical metaphors to describe growth. Rostow's and other theories of prerequisites are described as "beautiful exercises in logic" (101; cf. 100, middle) which "have been defeated by history."

Gerschenkron's hypothesis about European industrialization is best described by dropping the language of "hypothesis" and using instead that of storytelling. The Bulgarian experience, for example, "rejects" the hypothesis, because Bulgaria's rate of industrial growth "was obviously far below what one should expect in view of the country's degree of backwardness" (126; cf. 1962d, 232). He notes that Bulgaria frittered away its governmental entrepreneurship on military adventures. In the "failures" of the story one's attention is drawn to illuminating facts. In the peroration of *Europe in the Russian Mirror* he specifically rejects the language of hypothesis testing even while using it:

For in trying to set up interpretative models [*read "stories"*] historians do not deal in universal propositions which can never be verified and can only be refuted [*a direct attack on modernist dogma*]. We deal in particular or existential propositions. It is the very nature of an historical hypothesis [*back to modernism: read "plot"*] to constitute a set of expectations which yields enlightenment . . . within a spatially and temporally limited zone. To determine the delimitations of that zone does not mean at all a refutation of a hypothesis [*if "hypothesis" is not understood in its modernist sense*], but on the contrary its reinforcement as a tool of historical understanding. (1970, 130)

The last sentence makes no sense if relative backwardness is a "hypothesis" like the inverse square law. If planets were attracted to each other inversely in proportion to the *cube* of the distance between them, that would be that. There would be no sense in which such a contrary finding "would not necessarily detract from my approach" (130). Relative backwardness, however, is not a scientific hypothesis in the folk philosopher's sense, but a device for telling a story, like the notion of the frontier in American history or the notion of the bourgeois revolutions of the late eighteenth century or the notion of progress in biological evolution or the notion of wrinkling through cooling in the geology of mountains. Relative backwardness can be proven wrong (as the scientific notions just mentioned mainly have been) if it violates the sense of reasoned adequacy.

By now I do not have to argue in detail that storytelling is not unscientific. Plate tectonics is a story, not a universal hypothesis like the inverse square law or the Schrödinger equation. Better yet, and more conformable with Gerschenkron's delight in botanical analogies, the theory of evolution is a story. Determining the delimitations of evolution does not mean at all "refuting the hypothesis." Anti-evolutionists think they refute evolution by taking seriously the falsificationist claims of folk philosophy. Scientists who mix amateur philosophy of science with incompetent anthropology of religion can expect no mercy from the Arkansas legislature. Not admitting that science itself uses techniques of storytelling is a strategic mistake. As a "hypothesis" (*Oxford English Dictionary*, 1933, definition 3) evolution is a failure because it is in modernist terms "meaningless." But by the standard of reasoned adequacy it is of course a spectacular and continuing success.

The difference between a modernist "hypothesis" and this way of telling a story has been discussed by Gerschenkron's colleague and friend, Albert Hirschman, without reference to Gerschenkron though in a similar spirit. Hirschman, another product of an elite Continental education, for long a professor at the Institute for Advanced Study at Princeton and an economic advisor to the democracies of Latin America, is even more explicit than Gerschenkron was about the literary character of social thinking. He has brought a self-conscious use of language to economics. An essay of 1970 entitled "The Search for Paradigms as a Hindrance to Understanding"—the title captures what irritated Gerschenkron about Marx and Rostow—complained that solely metaphorical thinking has made "Latin American societies seem somehow less complex and their 'laws of movement' more intelligible, their medium-term future more predictable," than societies north of the border (1979 [1970], 170f)]. He commended instead a storytelling mode:

This view of large-scale social change as a unique, nonrepeatable, and *ex ante* highly improbable complex of events is obviously damaging to the aspirations of anyone who would explain and predict these events through "laws of change." . . . There is no denying that such "laws" or paradigms can have considerable utility. They are . . . indispensable devices for achieving a beginning of understanding after the event has happened. That is much, but that is all. The architect of social change can never have a reliable blueprint. Not only is each house he builds different from any other that was built before, but it also necessarily uses new construction materials and even experiments with untested principles of stress and structure. (179)

The story in other words is a form of knowledge no less dignified for science than is the metaphor. Projecting metaphors into the future without the discipline of storytelling is dangerous. As Gerschenkron said, the beautiful exercises in logic are often enough defeated by history.

A rhetorical reading of Gerschenkron does not reveal him as a non-scientist, a mere word spinner. He shaped in his work a story of his own life, one of care and precision and attention to the words themselves. Master scientists are master rhetoricians, word spinners in no dishonorable sense, or else they do not win the argument. Gerschenkron's science was model building but also storytelling, using all of the rhetorical tetrad. And so in this instance again: Science is rhetoric, all the way down.

6 Metaphor Against the Story: Chaos and Counterfactuals

*B*ut all is not well. Some stories are good, some bad, as an adult needs hardly to be told. Their goodness or badness can be tested against the other parts of the rhetorical tetrad, against the facts, the logics, and the metaphors.

Facts of course constrain a story. The fish in the fisherman's story was either a lake bass or a sunfish, and that's that. The empiricist tradition since Bacon has put great emphasis on facts testing stories. No one could object, though it would be miraculous if there was anything new to say about the empiricist tradition. What is valuable in the tradition can be preserved to do its good work even if one thinks that scientific argument involves more still. The philosophically inclined need not at this point commence kicking stones and pounding tables to show that facts are facts and therefore all we need. Thinking of science as also involving stories and metaphors does not require skepticism about facts. The facts are there, killing the story or giving it life.

The story is made by people, the facts are made by God; but of course we need both to make sense. It is like fishing. We humans make the lures to catch the fish in the lake, but the fish are there by God's command, "really" there. We can believe trustingly that the fish are there even when our backs are turned, yet still admit that the design of the lures is a human job. Or we can believe skeptically that the fish are after all themselves fish by human construction (is a guppy a fish?), yet admit that the world's best lure trailed through a lake without something we call fish would not catch any. So facts criticize stories.

Logic, too, criticizes stories, of course. The rationalist tradition since Descartes has put great emphasis on the internal consistency of stories. Again no one objects. The exact meaning of "logical" constraints on stories is elusive, though perhaps the rule that two contradictory events cannot take place simultaneously is an example, equivalent to A and not-A being mutually exclusive; or perhaps the sequence of time should be put down as logic, in which the future cannot affect the past.

The other criticism of stories, and the point here, arises from the last of the tetrad, metaphors. The criticism goes both ways. Metaphors criticize stories and stories criticize metaphors. A metaphor of modern economic growth—as an airplane taking off, for example—can conflict with a story—of varied saving rates in the "great spurt," for example, depending on the previous history of backwardness. The conflict between a metaphor and a story about the economy fits under the rhetorical theory of commonplaces. Commonplaces are the arguments ready to hand about which we converse in science and ordinary life. The psychologist Michael Billig gives in this connection the example of proverbs, "Many hands make light work" as against "Too many cooks spoil the soup" (1989, 298). The two contradict each other. Is it light work or too many cooks? The ordinary deliberations of life, and of science, are like this, and the contradictions are nothing pathological. The fruitful contradiction among figures of speech is itself a commonplace of argument.

Metaphors sometimes contradict stories, and sometimes not so fruitfully. Sharon Kingsland writes about the history of population biology that "the use of models to construct plausible scenarios . . . is in its ahistorical character opposed to the way of thinking familiar to most ecologists. The difficulty of trying to reconcile these two ways of thinking has been the source of much controversy" (1985, 5). We talk about the causes of events, such as the Great Depression or the American Civil War. Economists will talk in metaphors; historians will talk in stories. But the two speak against one another. The very idea of cause in a story can be left in doubt.

A recent book by the economist and historian Robert Fogel, *Without Consent or Contract: The Rise and Fall of American Slavery* (1989), argues that there was nothing inevitable about Lincoln's election and the resulting secession. Like many historians before him he emphasizes the precarious balance of American politics in the 1850s, which could have been turned one way or the other by minor events. In the late 1850s:

> The Republican party was not wrecked by the panic of 1857 and by 1860 it had lured most of the former Know-Nothings into its ranks. However, neither outcome was inevitable. . . . It is doubtful that party leaders could have continued to suppress the nativist impulses of so many of its members if immigration had returned to the 1854 rate. . . . If the party would have conceded these demands, some of the Germans and the more conservative Whigs would have been alienated. Only relatively small defections were needed to deny power to the anti-slavery coalition in 1860. (385–86)

And during the fateful month of May 1856 in bloody Kansas:

> However, a sheriff who had proprietory interests in a rival town not far from Lawrence, and who was an impulsive extremist, took unauthorized command of the posse. The mob that he led burned the hotel that served as the headquarters for the New England Emigrant Aid Society. . . . Two days later, in retaliation for the "sack of Lawrence," John Brown and his sons killed "five helpless and unprepared pro-slavery settlers." . . . As the posse moved toward Lawrence, Senator Charles Sumner (R, MA) delivered a searing indictment . . . of leading Democratic members of the Senate, including Stephen A. Douglas (D, IL) and Andrew P. Butler (D, SC). Butler was absent from the chamber during Sumner's speech but Preston S. Brooks, a relative and a member of the House from South Carolina, brooded over the insults to his aged kinsmen and to his state. . . . Brooks entered the Senate chamber after it adjourned on May 22 and delivered a series of blows to Sumner's head and shoulders with his cane. (379)

Fogel identifies other turning points, too. He is trying to show that the end of slavery was by no means determined by massive and unstoppable forces, such as its alleged unprofitability or its alleged inconsistency with industry. "The overarching role of contingent circumstances in [the] ultimate victory [of the antislavery movement] needs to be emphasized. There never was a moment between 1854 and 1860 in which the triumph of the antislavery coalition was assured" (322).

James McPherson's recent history of the same era provides military examples. "The third critical point came in the summer and fall of 1863 when Gettysburg, Vicksburg, and Chattanooga turned the tide toward ultimate northern victory" (1988, 858). Vicksburg was settled by many things—one is put in mind of the much-abused term "over-determination"—but among them was a disagreement before the siege between the Confederate generals Joe Johnston and John C. Pemberton.

Johnston urged Pemberton to unite his troops with Johnston's 6,000 survivors north of Jackson [Mississippi], where with expected reinforcements they would be strong enough to attack Grant. . . . Pemberton disagreed. He had orders to hold Vicksburg and he intended to do so. . . . Before the two southern generals could agree on a plan, the Yankees made the matter moot by slicing up Pemberton's mobile force on May 16 at Champion's Hill. (630)

At Gettysburg one of numerous turning points was the desperate defense of Little Round Top on July 2 by colonel Joshua L. Chamberlain of the 20th Maine. Chamberlain (who not incidentally was in civilian life a professor of rhetoric) ordered his men, ammunition exhausted, to attack with bayonets the massing Confederates down the hill. "The two Round Tops dominated the south end of Cemetery Ridge. If the rebels had gotten artillery up there, they could have enfiladed the Union left. . . . Shocked by the audacity of this bayonet assault, the Alabamians surrendered by scores to the jubilant boys from Maine" (659).

In the conclusion to his book McPherson writes, "Northern victory and southern defeat in the war cannot be understood apart from the contingency that hung over every campaign, every battle, every election, every decision during the war. This phenomenon of contingency can best be presented in a narrative format" (858). Precisely. Fogel and McPherson are telling the usual story: For want of a nail, the shoe was lost; for want of a shoe, the horse was lost; . . . for want of the battle, the kingdom was lost, and all for the want of a horseshoe nail.

Little events can have big consequences in some parts of the history. The parts are described by models that are nonlinear in the events and whose consequences feed on themselves. That is, a little event stuck affecting one of the equations yields a large consequence, which is then fed back as input. "Nothing succeeds like success" is such a model, and certainly applies to the decade 1856–65 in the United States.

The point is not that great oaks from little acorns grow. They do, as did Christianity and the Industrial Revolution, and the right acorn is impossible to see before the event. Any one of numberless acorns may be chosen by chance. Chance of this conventional sort is similarly difficult to narrate. But at least after the acorn is chosen it grows smoothly from acorn to sprout to sapling to tree, shaped by the great forces of its environment. The point here is rather that in some modeled worlds an acorn produces by itself a great tree in an instant. Such a world is instable. The models need not be complicated. As students of "chaos theory" have pointed out, simple models can generate astonishingly complicated patterns in which the slightest perturbation can yield an entirely different history. Confederate success depended on recognition by Great Britain, which depended on . . . Confederate success. It depended on human wills at Lawrence, Kansas or Little Round Top.

What of it? The problem is that in such a world the idea of storytelling is cast into doubt. In the opinion of two careful students, American history 1856–65 was in such a precarious state that even small events could have a big effect. The rogue sheriff and the bold professor of rhetoric "changed history," as we say. But in that case *any* of an unbounded set of little people and little events could be brought into the story. Unknown to history, a certain John Jones in Kansas, who alone had the moral authority to stop the sheriff, failed to arrive in the posse (he had a cold and was in bed). Likewise unknown to history, a political general named Robert Smith in 1861 had assigned Chamberlain to the 20th Maine quite by accident—Chamberlain should have been put in the 21st, not the 20th, but it was late at night when Smith did the job, and the orders had to go out by the next morning, leaving no time to check them.

In some counterfactual world the Civil War and its outcome might have been governed by big, simple, linear metaphors—slavery might have been steadily less profitable despite southern sentiments, the North might have been destined to win despite southern generalship. The success of Christianity, likewise, depended on the Roman Empire, and the Industrial Revolution on the freedoms of northwestern Europe. But if, as Fogel and McPherson and many historians before them have persuasively argued, the correct models for 1856–65 are models of nonlinear feedback then the story becomes unmanageable, untellable. It is a paradox.

The paradoxes that can arise from a story linked with a metaphor become most evident in the notion of a "counterfactual." Counterfactuals are the what-ifs, the thought experiments, the alternatives to actual history. They imagine what would have happened to any army, family, or economy if, contrary to fact, something in the army, family, or economy had changed. What if Representative Preston Brooks in 1856 had kept his temper and stayed his cane? What if Chamberlain in 1863 had not charged from Little Round Top? If Cleopatra's nose had been a half inch longer would the battle of Actium have been fought? If railroads had not been invented would American national income have grown much slower than it did?

The philosophical (and grammatical) literature speaks of counterfactuals as "contrary-to-fact conditionals." The notion has been used most self-consciously in historical economics. For example: "If railroads had not been invented the national income of the United States would have been at most a few percentage points lower." But counterfactuals are implied in many other parts of economics, such as macroeconomics: "If a rule of money growth at 2 percent a year were adopted then the rate of inflation would fall"; or industrial organization: "If the instant camera industry had 100 manufacturers then it would be a competitive industry."

The rhetorical problem that counterfactuals raise, and part of the reason they have attracted the attention of philosophers, can be seen in the last example. You want to compare the present monopoly of instant cameras—Kodak lost a suit some time ago about its patents on instant cameras and Polaroid since then has made and sold them all—with (nearly) perfect competition. You might want to do so in order to measure the cost of monopoly and to advise a judge in court. You want to know what is the significance of the monopoly, and such knowledge requires a counterfactual.

Now of course if somehow the instant camera industry were to have 100 sellers then each seller would be small relative to the whole demand or supply. Speaking technically, the elasticity of the demand curves facing any one seller would be on the order of 100 times the elasticity of total demand. Such calculations are the heart of applied economics. If the cigarette tax were raised what would happen to the price of cigarettes? If the money supply were increased what would happen to the general level of prices? If foreign doctors could practice freely in the United States what would happen to the cost of American medical care?

Such questions involve looking into a world having, say, an instant camera industry with 100 sellers rather than one. Such a world would not be ours. How then is the counterfactual to be imagined? By what allegory combining metaphor and story? And do the metaphor and story coexist with ease?

The rhetorical problems which can afflict counterfactuals are two: vagueness and absurdity. The vagueness arises when the metaphor used to extrapolate into the not-world is vague. The metaphor is the model. The not-world could arrive at 100 companies selling instant cameras in many different ways. For example, one could imagine getting 100 Polaroid companies by fragmenting edict now, in the style of the breakup of American Telephone and Telegraph Company. The advantages of greater competition would have to be set against the disadvantages. A breakup now would change the patent law in the future, since no one would expect the breakup of Polaroid to be the last breakup. A patent law that did not allow Polaroid to take advantage of its past cleverness in tying up the technology would change the economy for good or ill. A world in which patents were granted and then abrogated is different from the present world. To imagine it one needs a non-vague model of what would happen to inventive activity.

Alternatively one might imagine subsidies in the 1940s that would have resulted originally in 100 alternative technologies for instant cameras (in fact only two were ever developed commercially, Polaroid's and then Kodak's). Such a counterfactual would have its own costs, again by changing the expectations of inventors. A counterfactual requires a metaphor broad enough to extrapolate confidently into the not-world.

Vagueness, in other words, is solved by explicitness in metaphors. Once made explicit the metaphors can be tested for their aptness. Since the 1960s historical economists have made extensive use of such extrapolations into the not-world, riding a model out into the darkness (McClelland 1975). In the most famous use of counterfactuals that same Robert Fogel (1964) calculated what the transport system of the United States in 1890 would have looked like without the railroads. He argued that evaluating the "indispensability" of the iron horse entailed calculating what American life would have been like without it. Some historians balked at the counterfactual saying that it was "'as if' history, quasi-history, fictitious history—that is not really history at all . . . , a figment" (Redlich 1970 [1968], 95 f). But economists find the notion natural, and philosophers accept it as routine.

The philosophers note that all of the following are nearly equivalent (see Goodman 1965, 44):

SCIENTIFIC LAW: *All inflations arise from monetary growth.*

CAUSAL ASSERTION: *Money growth alone causes inflation.*

FACTUAL CONDITIONAL: *Since inflation has changed, money growth has changed.*

DISPOSITIONAL STATEMENT: *Inflation is controllable with money growth.*

PARALLEL WORLDS: *In a world identical to ours (or sufficiently similar) except that money growth differed, inflation would be different.*

COUNTERFACTUAL: *If money growth were to be held at zero, then inflation would be zero as well.*

The philosophy of counterfactuals revolves around the translation of one of these into another. Non-philosophers seldom recognize that the translations are possible. Historians for example flee in terror from the counterfactual, as contrary to the rhetoric of Fact in their discipline, and cling stoutly to their causal statements. Economists have the opposite philosophical neurosis, clinging to counterfactuals—in their rhetoric, Theory, the metaphors that nourish economics—and fleeing causal statements, which they regard, strangely, as unscientific. Both believe that the thing itself can be avoided by avoiding its name.

Fogel's calculation stirred great controversy, but was robust to criticism (1979). He was interested in long-term growth, and therefore did not posit a sudden closure of the railroads in 1890. A sudden closure would clearly have driven national income down sharply. (Mental experiments of the sudden-closure type are what lie behind claims that railroads or airlines or agriculture or garbage collection are "essential.") Fogel imagined instead what the American economy would have looked like without access to railroads right from the beginning, forced from the 1830s onward to rely on substitutes like roads or canals, or manage with less transport. Such an economy would have made better roads and would have dug more canals. It would have located production and consumption closer together and both closer to natural waterways. It would have had a larger St. Louis and a smaller Denver.

Fogel did not specify every feature of the "true" counterfactual world. He did not for example suppose that the internal combustion engine would have been perfected earlier, as it probably would have in a railroadless world. He was trying to show that the railroad was not so important, and therefore biased the case against himself, allowing the counterfactual world to adjust only in a few ways: for example, Denver in his world is no smaller. The result was a calculable *upper bound* on the value of railroads—an upper bound because had the world been allowed to adjust as it actually would have, the hurt from not letting it have the railroad would have been smaller. The upper bound was in 1890 about 5 percent of national income, only two years of economic growth. The greatest invention of the nineteenth century accounted for only a small part of economic growth, at most.

Fogel was merely applying in a bold way the usual method of economics. The usual method is the poetics of economics, imagining an explicit economic model, M, with parameters, P, and initial conditions or outside variables, I, and the resulting values of the outcomes, R. The counterfactual then imagines a change in some element of the model. The simplest is a variation in I, where I might be a tax rate in a model of cigarette consumption or the number of firms in a naive model of instant camera pricing. Fogel removed from the initial conditions one of the technologies of transportation. In similar fashion a 500-equation model of the American economy allows economists to look into alternative worlds. What would happen to American prosperity if the price of oil rose? What would be the effect on the poor of a lower tax on capital gains? (The main test of Fogel's work was in fact a multi-equation model of the Midwest and West in the late nineteenth century constructed by Jeffrey Williamson [1974].)

The counterfactual is the first of two officially scientific ways that economists explore the world (a third, controlled experiment, is uncommon). The second is curve fitting, the comparative method, comparing differing true stories as they exist in the world. It asks how *in fact* the results have varied in response to differing initial conditions. The counterfactual, or simulation with a metaphor, asks how the results *would* vary. The counterfactual is in the conditional mood ("If the demand for transport in Illinois in the 1850s can be represented by a curve . . . "). The curve fitting is in the indicative ("Once upon a time there were Illinois counties that had the railroad and others that did not"). The counterfactual infers R from data on P and from reflection on M and I. The curve fitting infers parameters P from data on initial conditions I and results R and from reflection on the model M.

But in solving the vagueness of a counterfactual by positing an explicit, metaphorical model the economist runs against the other rhetorical problem with counterfactuals: absurdity in the storytelling.

Consider again the counterfactual of a 100-firm industry selling instant cameras. In fact the implied story may violate the very model being used. The problem is that the initial conditions that would lead to a 100-firm industry may be absurd. The counterfactual assertion "If the instant camera industry were perfectly competitive then the price would be lower than it is now" sounds routine. But it can have the character of the proverbial absurdity "If my grandmother had wheels she'd be a tram." The metaphor or model may be true—wheeled grandmothers may indeed be trams—but the counterfactuals may be impossible. The counterfactual may contradict the very model used; or it may contradict some wider model of how things work. Such as: grandmothers do not develop wheels; 100-firm industries do not invent and produce instant cameras.

It is possible to argue on such grounds that *all* counterfactuals are absurd. One might argue, as did Leibnitz, that a world that did not invent the railroad would strictly speaking have to be a world different from our own world right back to the Big Bang. Such a world might be one in which seas were boiling hot or pigs had wings, with different problems of transportation. The wider theory violated by any counterfactual is that the world hangs tightly together. As John Stuart Mill remarked in attacking counterfactual comparisons of free trade and protection, "Two nations which agreed in everything except their commercial policy would agree also in that" (1872, 572).

The Norwegian political scientist Jon Elster, in a penetrating discussion of the role of counterfactuals in economic argument (1978), posed the Basic Paradox of Counterfactuals. The less vague the theory, the more likely is a counterfactual using the theory to become absurd. If Fogel had developed a theory of invention to draw a less vague picture of road transport he would have faced the problem that the very theory would have predicted the invention of railroad. It had better. Railroads, after all, *were* invented. As Elster put it, "If he attempted to strengthen his conclusion . . . he would be sawing off the branch he is sitting on. In this kind of exercise it is often the case that more is less and that ignorance is strength" (206). The counterfactual must be, as Elster says, "capable of insertion into the real past." That is, the model must fit the story. But the more explicit the metaphor the more difficult it is to insert into the actual story of the past.

A mix of metaphor and story is an allegory, a narrative of "one coherent set of circumstances which signify a second order of correlated meanings" (Abrams 1981, 6). *The Pilgrim's Progress* is based on correlated metaphors such as a voyage to the Heavenly City = spiritual progress; and Christian = all men who would be saved. Yet it is not a merely timeless model but a story, too, in which Christian attains the City and loses his burden of sin. Any rich account of a real economy is going to be allegorical, requiring its stories and metaphors to coexist. The point is that they coexist uneasily.

Metaphor and story are not merely alternate ways of explaining; in a conversation of allegory, in which both must function, they can contradict each other. As the critic Northrop Frye noted in this connection, the symbol in modern literature, such as Melville's white whale or Samuelson's utility function, is a metaphor that stops short of full (naive) allegory. The symbol "is in a paradoxical and ironic relation to both narrative and meaning [to storytelling and metaphor making, in other words]. As a unit of meaning [that is, as a metaphor], it arrests the narrative; as a unit of narrative, it perplexes the meaning" (1957, 92).

The Basic Paradox illuminates a long controversy in economics about the simplicity of models. One group of economists favors simple models because they are more understandable; another group favors complex models because they are more complete. Both may be wrong. A simpler model is harder to believe in counterfactual experiments because it is not rich. But because it is not rich it is more likely to be insertable into the past—that is, it is less likely to result in absurd contradictions of what we already know in a storytelling way (that railroads were in fact invented, for example). By contrast, a 500-equation model of the American economy will more tightly constrain the story into which it is inserted than the 10-equation model. The selection of stories and metaphors is subject, like most things, to scarcity.

Synchronic, metaphoric models, if pushed, produce history contrary to fact; diachronic narratives, if pushed, contradict synchronic models we all know to be true. That is the nub of the issue. When a metaphor is used too boldly in telling a history it becomes ensnared in logical contradictions, such as those surrounding counterfactuals. If a model of an economy imagines what would have happened without the industrial revolution, then the contradiction is that an economy of the British sort did in fact experience an industrial revolution. Oh, oh. A world in which the Britain of 1780 did not yield up an industrial revolution would have been a different one before 1780, too. The model wants to imagine a different future without imagining a different past. It wants to eat the cake and have the ingredients, too. It contradicts the actual story of how Britain came to 1780 and beyond.

Likewise, when a mere story attempts to predict something by extrapolation into the future it contradicts some persuasive model. The story of business cycles can organize the past, but it contradicts itself when offered as a prediction of the future. All manner of stage theories of business cycles have this difficulty. If the stories of past business cycles could predict the future there would be no surprises, and by that fact no business cycles. Any model of business cycles must talk of people predicting badly: of bankers thinking that the boom is going to continue one month longer than it does, of auto makers investing in a big, new plant just before their sales drop. But if business cycles are unpredictable to the actors they are unpredictable to the drama critics, too. The extrapolated story contradicts a model.

Whatever difficulties a story faces in the light of a model, or a model in light of a story, economists use both. Like other human beings they use the phrases "just like this" and "once upon a time" routinely for their work. Economists are concerned both to explain and to understand. (They are concerned also, of course, to confront and to deduce: they use facts and logic, too.) Economists, that is, are allegorists. They have the same problem as the religious allegorists, such as John Bunyan the Puritan. If Christian in *The Pilgrim's Progress* is a model of fallible humanity then the ending is not credible, since no such man would obtain salvation. But if the story holds then the metaphor is wrong. Only a miracle of grace can save a sinner, and save the allegory of *The Pilgrim's Progress*. Only a miracle of intellectual compromise can fit the static model of maximization into the story of capitalist success.

Stories criticize metaphors and metaphors criticize stories. A story told through a nonlinear metaphor will break down into absurd detail. A counterfactual metaphor carried too far will absurdly violate the story of the past. But these are not knockdown arguments, merely doubts that the allegory of self-interest in economics can always bring its metaphor and its stories together. We make the stories and metaphors and are therefore unable to appeal to God's certainty in judging which one is best or how they should be combined. We must talk about them, trying one against the other in human conversation.

7 The Poetics and Economics of Magic

W hen the metaphors do battle with the story, the result is nonsense, nonsense that can hurt when people believe it. People do. People especially believe in allegories, such as the combined metaphors and stories of economics, because an allegory in its completeness protects the illusion of prediction and control. The chemistry of snake oil is allegorical.

Around 1600 in England it was reported that "among the common people he is not adjudged any scholar at all, unless he can tell men's horoscopes, cast out devils, or hath some skill in soothsaying" (Thomas 1971, 227). Nowadays the press and public commonly treat the economist as a soothsayer (albeit a dubious one), to the point of believing that economics aims mainly at forecasting. The economist sometimes obliges, bemused by the physics-as-philosophy promise of prediction and control.

But the forecasting of human events—which is *not* the main activity of economics—has always been magical. In human affairs there is prediction but no profitable prediction, and therefore no perfectly reliable control. "The unscrawled fores the future casts," sings Wallace Stevens of impending death, is "damned hoobla-hoobla-hoobla-how" ("Notes Towards a Supreme Fiction: It Must Be Abstract, II," in Stevens 1972; Stevens, who read Latin well, puns the nonce-plural of fore-, as in *fore*casting, with Latin *fore* = *futurus esse* = "to be about to be," from which "the about-to-bes" = the future; and perhaps also Latin *fores* = the double doors in the poet's bedroom through which the moonlight scrawls. Harold Bloom draws out the erotic reference in the deliberate variation of hoobla-*how*—that is, *how* can a man of 63 bring back the life of Venus's dove, hoobla-hooing in the day?—but does not comment on the magic [Bloom 1976, 180–82]).

Forecasting the future seems at first more scientific and grown-up than the mere casting of spells, which commands carpets to fly or Daddy to drop dead. But forecasting the future and manipulating it are identically magical. The desire to forecast the future and the desire to change it are two sides of the same desire. The one forecasts the future from the flights of birds or the entrails of chickens, and is armed by the forecast to prevent evil. The other, less prestigious, knows already the future evil and arms itself with magic spells and amulets to prevent it.

It is superstitious to think that profitable forecasts about human action are easily obtainable. That is why economics, contrary to the common sneer, is not mere magic and hoobla-hoo. Economics itself says that forecasts, like many other desirable things, are scarce. It cannot be easy to know which great empire will fall or when the market will turn. "Doctor Friedman, what's going to happen to interest rates next year?" Hoobla-hoo. Some economists allow themselves to be paid cash to answer such questions, but they know they can't. Their very science says so.

The subject, then, is the economics of magic—not sleight of hand but real magic. Real magic claims to have solved scarcity. It leaps over the constraints of the world. If you desire a ride to Baghdad, here is a magic carpet; if you desire your enemy dead, here is a magic doll; if you desire unlimited riches, here is a forecast of interest rates. As the expressive jargon of economics puts it, magic leaps outside our "production possibilities." The "fiat" in a spell is the desire to get outside what is ordinarily possible. The magic of course begins with desire. Stevens again:

> But the priest desires. The philosopher desires.
> And not to have is the beginning of desire.
> To have what is not is its ancient cycle.

It is desire at the end of winter, when
It observes the effortless weather turning blue.

("Notes: Abstract, II")

Stevens points to the desire motivating both childish magic and adult arts and sciences, a desire which notes the "effortless" turning of seasons, and dreams therefore of similar power for itself, "pure power," the achieving without effort. An economist would call the desire a "utility function" or, less fancily, "tastes." People have a taste for going to Baghdad free of charge or have a taste for avoiding the bad luck from breaking a mirror (the term is "apotropaic" magic, averting magic). Fear of the future motivates economic advising. The hiring of economists by politicians and businesspeople otherwise hardnosed is apotropaic.

The grown-up way to satisfy the desire to avoid evil or achieve riches is to work within the world's limitations and satisfy it. Robinson Crusoe did not spend time casting spells (though he mourned a while), but stripped the wreck and built a stockade, reinventing the arts and sciences and retraining his desires. Children desire that avoiding evil or achieving riches were not so hard, a desire that is father to the thought. Children think that if they wish hard enough it will be so: "Let Daddy *die*." In his old classic on the sociology of magic, Marcel Mauss noted that "between a wish and its fulfillment there is, in magic, no gap" (1972 [1902–3], 63). A small child believes in the omnipotence of thought, as Freud put it, because he has not yet distinguished his private dreams from the collective dreams we name reality. Adults who cannot make such distinctions are said to be mentally ill.

In *Ancient Egyptian Magic* Bob Brier describes the pharaoh before a sea battle sinking toy models of enemy ships in his bathtub (1980, 51). Real magic, as distinct from the parlor trick, depends often on such a metonymy, taking a thing associated with X as *being* X. It re-presents what the magician wishes to happen. Actually, the pharaoh reminds an economist of advisors representing an economy with a model, then sinking the deficit in the bathtub.

An important magical power of words is naming. Metonymic ("other-name") magic, like the pharaoh's toy boats or the voodoo priest's dolls, reduces the thing to an object, or more conveniently to a word, and then works. Knowing the name of the man to be cursed puts him in the magician's power. "The deep tradition of efficacious words" in poetry and magic, notes the critic Hugh Kenner, "stems from an authority of naming" (1987, 16–17). Joyce's *Dubliners* was unprintable not because it used the word "bloody" but because it named actual pubs in the town, the names "frozen in the eerie finality of type," and doubly dangerous (28). Giving each American soldier a nameplate has a deeper purpose than providing introductions for the lonely crowd. In Vietnam one night a young white lieutenant faced alone a room of black enlisted men, properly nameplated, like him. Noticing that he had no business there, he edged towards the door. One of the nameplated soldiers blocked the way: "You're in trouble sir." The lieutenant gathered his nerve, braced, flipped his lapel to show his own plate, and snarled as he pushed out the door, "You remember my name, son, because I'm sure as hell going to remember yours." The nameplate worked its magic.

The power of naming illustrates the drift of the signifier towards the signified. We symbol-using animals like to name things. After a while we get to thinking that having their names is as good as having the things themselves. British people learn to name the flora of their pleasant land down to each wild flower on the verge, giving them a mastery foreign to Americans. The Russian poet and critic Andrey Bely wrote that "The process of naming . . . is a process of invocation. Every word is a charm. By charming a given phenomenon I am in essence subjugating it. . . . For living speech itself is unbroken magic. . . . The word ignites the gloom surrounding me with the light of victory" (1985 [1909], 94f.).

But the victories through words and names, of course, are cheap. This is the economic problem with magic. If mere saying is enough and if the saying is not somehow restricted, then evil eyes proliferate. Thomas M. Greene, a professor of English and comparative literature at Yale, a student of Renaissance literature (and not entirely incidentally a passionate baseball fan), has articulated recently a theory of poetry which has parallels to economics (1989). The difficulty for the symbol-using animal is to use symbols without the "pressure of desire," Greene says, which allows the symbols to become a riot of magical, desire-granting charms. Bloom quotes Santayana, an influence on Wallace Stevens in "Notes towards a Supreme Fiction," to similar effect. Santayana defines poetry as being "religion [read magic] without practical efficacy and without metaphysical illusions" (Bloom 1976, 175). Or still better, poetry says so: it is, as Greene argues, perfectly aware that the age of miracles is past.

Economics also says that desires cannot be granted easily and that magic is without practical efficacy. A functionalist and sociological argument would be that a society filled with evil eyes could not function, and therefore would not exist. Magic-haunted societies in fact are often paralyzed by conflict, as Salem, Massachusetts was in the 1690s, which played with magic under children's rules. A society that is going to come to terms with the reality principle must somehow limit the omnipotence of thought.

More economistically one could argue that people will not put a high value on what is cheap. Magic must be more expensive than merely snapping one's fingers or else it will not be accounted powerful. To deal with uncertainty we need magic, and especially we need it when poor. The winners of the state lottery are mostly poor and naive. Again the magic cannot be too cheap. A valuable magical spell is believed, and therefore one way to get it believed is to make it expensive, boldly asserting its value. ESSL Corp (P. O. Box 66054, Los Angeles, CA 90066) sells the most expensive of six programs available from various companies to guess the next numbers of the lottery. The program sells not for its cost of production (a few dollars) or for its value in use (nothing) but for the persuasively substantial price of $59.95. Psychoanalysts require that the patient pay a lot, because otherwise the therapy will not work. The patient has to make a sacrifice to get well.

In other words—and this is the essential point—magic has to be expensive. The economic idea is called "rent-seeking." Magic promises something for nothing. It is like the government and like working for the government. We clever moderns know that magic does not work. If magic is to survive (this is a third functionalist argument) it must be made expensive or else people would complain that they snapped their fingers but still got sick. The rhetoric of magic demands that the magic be difficult to perform or else its failure to work will be too evident. Magic promises profit, the same way an economic forecast does. Therefore the business of magic will attract entry, at length driving down its profit. The argument is biological: ecological niches do not lie around unexploited. At length the costs of making the last bit of magic will equal its value in free rides to Baghdad or in daddies conveniently disposed of.

The character of magic fits the argument. The standard theory, that magic is the primitive man's science, is useful but not nuanced (although see Maddison 1982, chap. 3). As Keith Thomas remarks, the theory "does not of course make clear why magical rituals should take one form rather than another" (1971, 648). By contrast:

Magic is often practical. It is businesslike, not therapeutic or ornamental: it expects to work. It is therefore humorless. The rhetorical form is that of a speech in court, with exordium, narratio, refutatio, and conviction. By contrast, nothing follows immediately from a religious ceremony or a poetry reading or a proper economic analysis. People just go home. "It is small wonder that the sorcerer's claim to produce practical results should have so often proved more attractive than stern clerical insistence that all must be left to God's inscrutable mercies" (264). From a witch's sabbath all manner of evil follows at once.

Magic is often arrogant. No business here of "Thy will be done." The god or spirit is to leap to it and is to be punished if he does not. The fiat in a spell does not pray to God; it summons the powers. "Deer's Cry" (St. Patrick, attributed, c. A.D. 440) proceeds for some fifty lines of praise for God, looking like a hymn—a lyrical assertion of a faith suitably humble—revealing its magic only by repetition. But abruptly it gets to the magical point, proclaiming, "I *summon* to-day all these *powers*" (italics added), and then lists them in detail (among them the important powers "against spells of women and smiths and wizards").

Magic is often secret. Mauss argues that "religious rites are performed openly, in full public view, [but] magical rites are carried out in secret. . . . And even if the magician has to work in public he makes an attempt to dissemble, . . . [to] hide behind simulated or real ecstasies" (1972 [1902–3], 23). One can doubt Mauss's assurance that magical and religious ceremony are sharply different, yet agree that secrecy is common for the magical type. The secrecy makes for scarcity, no less than a secret recipe for baking bread or a secret method for casting iron thin enough for pots.

Magic is often exclusive. "Nobody can become a magician at will; there are qualities which distinguish a magician from the layman" (27). Again the economics works to raise the price. The list of candidates for magical powers must be restricted to make it expensive. As Socrates says in his elitist way, "not everyone is an artisan of names, but only he who keeps in view the name which belongs by nature to each particular thing" (Plato, *Cratylus* 390E). The expert can see into the mind of God, being "a master of name giving" (389D). The candidate for magician must be unusual in some way. Smiths, barbers, shepherds, foreigners, infidels, primitives, and other special, lonely people can become magicians (Mauss 1972 [1902–3], 28ff.), meaning that one man's tribe is another's league of sorcerers. The Jews were thus steadily suspect of magic, and the Lapps could sell bags of wind to European sailors (32). Specialness, not rarity, is the key—for women were commonly magical (because excluded from religion and from science), and there are plenty of them. Keith Thomas speaks of the advantage Catholic priests had over Protestant ministers in appropriating magic in the sixteenth and seventeenth centuries: "precisely because the Church had its own magic . . . it frowned on that of others. . . . Set apart by his learning, his unique ritual power, and his official virginity, the priest was admirably qualified to be a key figure in the practice of popular magic" (1971, 274). A magician learns the language of the spirits, at large cost. He knows the words the gods speak (Mauss 1972 [1902–3], 38f; *Cratylus,* 391E; contrast 401A; and the gods loving a joke, 406C). The magician undergoes initiation. Any man can call spirits from the vasty deep, but only for a magician will they come when he does call for them.

Magic is often nontransferable: "[A] person who has bought a charm cannot dispose of it at will outside the contract" (43). The nontransferability of charms and curses is the more revealing because it contradicts another feature of magic, that charms and curses are *done,* as Thomas Greene puts it, irrevocable, rattling down the generations (thus the curse on the house of Pelops in the *Oresteia*). Magic is a speech act, but more like the speech act of marrying a couple than the speech act of promising to repay a loan. A marriage cannot be sold secondhand; a promise to repay can. A secondhand marriage ceremony would be a cheapened act, which is the point.

Magic is often particular and local. Certain days are efficacious, certain difficult circumstances must be achieved, and so forth (45f.). "If the Hindu magicians are to be believed, some of their rites could be practiced successfully only once every forty-five years" (46). Naturally: if magic could be done on any day, in any place, it would not have the scarcity that protects its claim of efficacy. There would be too much of it around, selling cheaply.

Above all, magic is often elaborate. It is notoriously so, hooblahoo, an image of mysterious wisdom won by toil. The rites can last hours or days or weeks. Magic is repetitious, covering every possibility—or else it does not work, since tiny failures to follow the prescription protect the magician from responsibility. "It is natural for a magician to take refuge behind questions of procedure and technicalities, to protect himself in case of failure in magical prowess" (50); cf. Thomas (1971, 641).

Magical ceremonies are usually more elaborate than religious ceremonies. The scarcity in religion is accomplished by a restricted priesthood and, especially, by the limited efficacy of the prayer, corresponding with the fiat in a spell. The Christian sects with less elaborate preparation for their priests expect less from prayer. The extreme cases are Amish priests chosen by biblical lot or Quakers with no priests at all. The sects that think that prayer works cheaply, every time, are regarded by mainstream religions as magical— for example, the cults of saints in the South of Italy or pentecostal sects in the United States.

The bargain with the gods in charms, spells, and religious sacrifices is a curious part of this, since it is usually small and cheap. People do not actually sacrifice much, except the time of the magician. Cheap entrails are all the god actually gets in blood sacrifice (Levy 1989). The rest is eaten by the humans. Thus in a Navaho chant, from a ceremony lasting many days, "I have made your sacrifice / *I have prepared a smoke for you*" (from The Night Chant, excerpted in Rothenberg 1985, 84). One would expect there to be a rule of equal scarcity in operation here. Cheap sacrifices would use elaborate ceremony by a restricted class of magicians or priests, to make the total costly. On the other hand, expensive sacrifices (human sacrifices especially) would be cheap and quick, contrary to what one might otherwise expect in view of the gravity of the matter. The sacrifice of Polyxena on the tomb of Achilles, "the shedding of human blood upon a grave, / where custom calls for cattle" (Euripides, *Hecuba*, line 262), the climax of the play, was short in the text and unelaborate in form (lines 520–80; compare Euripides, *Iphigenia in Aulis*, lines 1540–80).

Magic, then, is childish. Childishly it gives way to the pressure of desire. Scarcity is wished away.

But economics knows that scarcity cannot really, truly be wished away. The scarcity must show somewhere and shows in most features of magic. The supposed profit arising from the evaded scarcity gets absorbed. Economics says: At the margin the hoobla-hoo must absorb the profit from being able to take the magician to Baghdad on a carpet, if he could only get the damned thing running.

Now poetry, Thomas Greene argues, is something different from magic. We speak of the "magic" of poetry, but only in a manner of speaking, hyperbole by way of careless praise. Poems commonly allude to the forms of magic, but no one thinks they actually achieve its substance. For all the shared rhetoric—repetition, incantation, evocation—poems are not spells.

In fact, Greene argues that poetry is a way of getting beyond the childish omnipotence of thought. Poems look like spells, but undercut the fiat with intrusions of voice, doubts that it will work, hints of the poet's personality, and other post-magical sensibilities. Sappho pretends in "Prayer to Aphrodite" (1971, 144–45) to accomplish the same thing as the Egyptian love spell, but is notably less businesslike, more personal, less repetitive, more revealing. The poem claims to be a love charm, but is in fact a lyric poem. It tells, irrelevantly for the magic, that "you, Blessed One, smiling with your immortal face, asked what happened to me." It is pathetic, not arrogant: "do not crush my heart"; "come here, if ever in the past, hearing my cries of love from afar"; "I was begging you to come"; "my mad heart"; "my crushing cares." Likewise, Theocritus II, "The Spell," inserts the magic in a narrative worthy of Browning, filled with irony and self-expression. Poems have many voices (if only the poet's in addition to the narrator's), but a spell has only one [James Fairhall made this point to me]. The reader—and of course it is a reader, not an audience of the shaman's patients or the local anthropologist—is made to reflect on the poem's pseudomagic.

In a poem, says Greene, "the emergent self is acculturated; it learns the limits of its own power" (1989, 131); "the inchoate wish is *schooled:* it is taught to speak and it is taught to accept limitation" (142). Like a child's game, it is "an elementary lesson in resignation" (131). "Poems tend to be pseudo-rituals which teach the subject to settle for the absence of magical power (131). Stevens:

> From this the poem springs: that we live in a place
> That is not our own and, much more, not ourselves
> And hard it is in spite of blazoned days.

("Notes: Abstract, IV")

The commonplace of classical criticism—that art and in particular poetry imitates reality—is wrong. Poetry does not imitate reality; it imitates speech acts, especially magical ones: curses, invocations, apostrophes, praise, prayer. Every poet knows it.

The awareness of its own lack of effectiveness makes poetry grown-up and post-magical. Poetry recognizes that the words are not the things themselves. It is adult, not expecting to reproduce by mere human words the effortless magic of blue-turning spring. The reader of a book in "The House Was Quiet and the World Was Calm" "leaned above the page / Wanted to lean, wanted most to be / The scholar to whom his book is true." But Stevens is here to tell you that after all it is only wanting, not achieving; that the book is true merely to the scholar, not to the gods.

In view of how grim it is to be adult and economic and aware of scarcity it is not perhaps surprising to find in poetry, as Greene does, a ubiquitous "nostalgia for magic." Poetry sometimes looks back on a time of omnipotent thought:

> The poem refreshes life so that we share,
> For a moment the first idea . . .
> The poem, through candor, brings back a power again
> That gives a candid kind to everything.

("Notes: Abstract, III")

But only "for a moment," a "kind." Candid, gleaming white, it claims to be, / But still it's hoobla-hoo. / Nostalgia might lament the truth, / But after all it's true.

Economics as a science, like poetry, is a force of acculturation. It says: you can't get that. The churches of the sixteenth and seventeenth centuries, writes Thomas (1971, 278), put "strong emphasis upon the virtues of hard work and application," and "helped create a frame of mind which spurned the cheap solutions offered by magic, not just because they were wicked, but because they were too easy. Man was to earn his bread by the sweat of his brow." Like poetry, and unlike magic, economics in the century after Defoe dwelt on scarcity. It came to tell that all good things must be scarce in equilibrium, all magical opportunities used up. It tells us we must work by the sweat of our brows to achieve our desires. It tells us that we cannot be rich by snapping our fingers. And it tells us that individual morality does not assure civic morality. Such hard messages would have been perhaps too hard for earlier and less settled times.

Economics is the science of the post-magical age. Far from being "unscientific" or hoobla-hoo, it is deeply anti-magical. It keeps telling us that we cannot do it, that magic will not help. After magic, Greene argues, poetry is scattered, dissociative, disjunctive, many voiced (compare Bloom 1976, 168, describing Stevens as "the most advanced rhetorician in modern poetry and in his major phase the most disjunctive"). Irony and self-consciousness would fit any page of Keynes.

Economics, like poetry, however, exhibits sometimes the nostalgia for magic. There's the danger. Economics can go wrong and betray its post-magical sophistication by surrendering to what Greene calls the temptation of magic. If poetry surrenders we are perhaps not seriously damaged—although the poetry then stops performing its maturing function and can even rouse men to magical beliefs in, say, the white man's burden or some corner of a foreign field that is forever England. Such notions are mischievous enough. But an economics that is nostalgic for magic is radically dangerous.

Now of course words are in fact efficacious in economics, because markets live on the lips of men and women. Every economist knows this. Money is not a thing, it is an agreement. Corporations are not corporeal. Exchange is a conversation of bids and asks.

The economy depends today on the promises made yesterday in view of the expectations about tomorrow. We can in fact (and in word) create prosperity by declaring it to be just around the corner. One is tempted to conclude that economies, and economics, are "mere" matters of words, that announcing a five-year plan or a new economic policy is the same thing as achieving it, that words after all do have the magical power to make us safe and happy.

Grown-ups must resist the temptation. Grown-up economics is not voodoo but poetry. Or, to take other models of maturity, it is history, not myth; politics, not invective; philosophy, not dogma. A correct economics—which is to say, most of the rich conversation of economics since Adam Smith—is historical and philosophical, a virtual psychoanalysis of the economy, adjusting our desires to the reality principle. On this score Marxian and bourgeois economics can be similarly childish in giving in to temptation. A Marxian economist of an old-fashioned sort trumpeting the predictive power of Marxism makes the same childish error as does a badly educated mainstream economist thinking that the future of grain prices is predictable. A grown-up epigram would be: The point is to know history, not to change it. The best economic scientists, of whatever school, have never believed in profitable casting of the fores.

The useful category for criticizing modernist culture, in other words, is not science/non-science but magic/non-magic à la Greene. It was customary in modernist circles in the 1930s to identify the enemies of modernism with Nazism. But the truth is that the Nazis drew much of their power from a modernist science grown magical. The buildings and displays of Auschwitz put one in mind not of tarot cards and crystal balls but of modernist laboratories and industrial processes gone mad in an attempt to lay down the future. Likewise, when the modern historical sciences yield to the temptation of myth—the myth of national destiny, for example, or the myth of social engineering—they become silly and magical and dangerous. Proper, non-magical science is here to tell us what we cannot do without cost. It resists making the scientists into wizards. It will not sell the snake oil. The danger comes from the modern sentimentalist armed with a myth of science gloriously magical.

8   The American Question: If You're So Smart Why Ain't You Rich?

*U*nhappily, economics sometimes forgets its scientific duty and begins to promise magical stories, reversals of fortune to be had merely by paying attention to the local economist. The magic of physical engineering in our world has long nourished a wish for social engineering. The economist is supposed to provide it, by the magic of expertise.

Americans say they don't hold much with experts. As Harry Truman said, "An expert is someone who doesn't want to learn anything new, because then he wouldn't be an expert." Europeans admit a need for expertise to keep their class struggle going, to which the American response is a Bronx cheer. Though Nicholas Murray Butler, the president of Columbia University long ago, made the university an American refuge for experts, he said that they know more and more about less and less. By way of contrast the European next to Nicholas Murray in the roll of remarks, Samuel Butler the Younger, had little respect for pretension in general but plenty for the pretension of experts: "The public do not know enough to be experts, yet know enough to decide between them." And having decided the public follows their magical advice.

You don't say. The rhetoric of the New World abounds with deflations: "Look who's talking"; "Where do you get off?" "Who d'you think *you* are, Bub?" And from Maine to California the capitalistic, American democrat relishes that most American of sneers, that American Question: "If you're so smart why ain't you rich?"

111

Well, why ain't you? The American scholar suffers taunts unimaginable in Germany or France, for not meeting a payroll, for not coming down from the ivory tower, for not getting wet behind the ears of his smarty egg head. Come to think of it, though, if he's so gosh darn smart why *hasn't* he gotten rich?

The question cuts deeper than most intellectuals and experts care to admit. The test of riches is a perfectly fair one if the expertise claims to deliver actual riches, in gold or in glory. At a minimum the American Question should constrain expertise about gold, and the counterstory can therefore begin with economics. It goes further, though. The American Question embarrasses anyone claiming magical and profitable expertise who cannot show a profit, the historian second-guessing generals or the critic propounding a formula for art. He who is so smart claims a Faustian knowledge, "Whose deepness doth entice such forward wits / To practice more than heavenly power permits."

Begin with economics. Take it as an axiom of human behavior that people pick up $500 bills left on the sidewalk. The Axiom of Modest Greed involves no close calculation of advantage or large willingness to take a risk. The average person sees a quarter and sidles over to it (by experiment it has been found that Manhattanites will stoop for a quarter); he sees a $500 bill and jumps for it. The Axiom is not controversial. All economists subscribe to it, whether or not they "believe in the market" (as the shorthand test for ideology goes), and so should you.

Yet it has a distressing outcome, a dismal commonplace of adult life, a sad little Five-Hundred-Dollar-Bill Theorem:

> If the Axiom of Modest Greed applies, then today there exists no sidewalk in the neighborhood of your house on which a $500 bill remains.

Proof: By contradiction, if there had been a $500 bill lying there at time $T - N$, then according to the axiom someone would have picked it up before T, before today.

From this advanced scientific reasoning it is a short step to common sense. If a man offers advice on how to find a $500 bill on the sidewalk, for which he asks merely a nominal fee, the prudent adult declines the offer. If there really were a $500 bill lying there the confidence man would pick it up himself.

Such common sense is so obvious that confidence games must clothe themselves in a false rhetoric of self-interest. In the Pigeon Drop the victim (that is, the pigeon) is persuaded to part with his bank account by way of earnest money for a share in a bundle of money "found" on the sidewalk. He must be persuaded that the con men are asking for the earnest money only as self-interested protection against the pigeon himself absconding with the bundle. (After the con men have disappeared with his bank account he finds out that the bundle entrusted to his care is paper stacked between two $10 bills). Even pigeons don't believe that someone will present them with $500 out of the goodness of his heart.

The leading case is the scheme to get rich quick. A letter arrives announcing itself as "The World's Greatest Secret! Now you can learn how to receive 50,000 crisp $5 bills in the next 90 days. . . . A personal note from the originator of the plan," Edward L. Green. His surprising kindness is affirmed by Carl Winslow of Tulsa: "This is the only realistic money-making offer I've ever received. I participated because this plan truly makes sense!"

Common sense replies that the plan truly does not make sense, not any sense at all. Though the plan uses the rhetoric of mutual interest—believe me, fella, this deal's good for you and me both— it does not turn the rhetoric on itself. If Mr. Green had the secret of receiving 50,000 crisp $5 bills he would clue you in only if your one crisp $5 bill was good for the chain and good for Edward L. Green. But you have no reason beyond Mr. Green's assurances to think you are early in the chain. If you are not you send out money and get nothing in return. A child will subscribe to a chain letter— or a guaranteed investment in Civil War figurines or a set of presidential commemorative coins suitable for collectors—and expect to win; an adult will not. No one with experience of life believes Publisher's Clearing House when it writes "*Ms. Z. Smithh*, you have just won $250,000." The adult does not expect fortune to come unbidded and asks prudently "Why are they telling me this?" Prudence is suspicious of an offer equivalent to picking up a $500 bill. Except to the flocks of optimistic Americans who invest daily in chain letters and prize-winning magazine subscriptions, all this goes without saying.

Therefore the Bargains and Hot Tips and Special Deals For You Alone offered by over-friendly men with clammy handshakes at dog tracks and used-car lots do not tempt the prudent adult. Yet similar offers made outside a Damon Runyon setting seem plausible to respectable if greedy folk. The high-class pigeons come flocking to the con, eager to believe that Mr. Expert is about to give them free advice on how to make a million.

Economists, for example, are routinely asked at cocktail parties what is going to happen to the interest rate or the price of housing or the price of corn. People think that asking an economist about the future is like asking the doctor at the party about that chest pain. You get an expert to do his job free. Take corn. Any agricultural economist in the Midwest spends much of his airtime delivering expert opinion on what will happen next month to its price. Surely he must know, this expert, if anyone does. It would be poor news to be told that after all no one does know, or can.

An economist who claims to know what is going to happen to the price of corn, however, is claiming to know how to pick up $500. With a little borrowing on the equity of his home or his reputation for sobriety he can proceed to pick up $500 thousand, then $500 million, then more. Nothing to it. If an agricultural economist could predict the price of corn better than the futures market he would be rich.

Yet he does not put his money where his mouth is. He is not rich. It follows by strict implication that he is not so smart.

It may be objected that the profitmaking is risky and that professors of economics are cautious. Therefore they do not put their money where their mouths are, even though their mouths are working fine. The objection has the problem that the bet on the price of corn can be hedged, which is insurance. It is no bet. Someone who can outsmart the market on average even a little can make a lot of money simply, at no risk. No wonder: the opportunity to buy corn low and sell high, like the right to run a TV station in the 1960s or to import Toyotas in the 1980s, is like finding a $500 bill any time you want.

It may be objected that the profitmaking is complicated and that professors of economics are elaborately trained experts in the complexities. Therefore the $500 bill is not available to just anyone, only to them. The wizards earn merely what they are worth, the normal return to years of studying wizardry. This objection, too, has problems. The first is that the wizards are telling us about the future price of corn or bonds or housing at cocktail parties and in the newspaper, free. Why are they handing over to John Doe their just rewards for going to wizard school?

The second problem is that the wizardry claimed is systematic, formulaic, and, when you come right down to it, pretty simple. It involves the fitting of a few straight lines to scatters of points. Take a course in economic statistics, the promise goes, and become able to predict the future in profitable ways. The promise is hard to believe, because it sounds a lot like The World's Greatest Secret. Ordinary secrets and routine advice do in fact flow from economics, and doubtless economists earn their keep. Unlimited wealth, however, cannot be expected to flow from a book or even from many years of concentrated study in economics. Compared to unlimited wealth, many years of study is like the trivial cost of reaching down to pick up a $500 bill. If someone knows a scholarly formula for predicting the price of corn it would already have been exploited.

The same grim truth from the American Question applies to the stock market. Because the stock market is obviously a matter of expectations, about which we all know something, and because it is crowded with experts in handsome wool suits, the truth is hard to swallow. Heh, *Barron's* and "Wall Street Week" wouldn't kid me, would they? Surely all those analysts and pundits and technical elves know *something*.

No, no, unhappily, they surely do not. They truly do not make sense; not any sense at all. The reason they do not is the American Question and the Five-Hundred-Dollar-Bill Theorem: there exists no sidewalk in your neighborhood with $500 of stock market profits lying on it. If a stockbroker were so smart he would not be making his riches by selling stock tips to widows and orphans. In the style of the chain letter, the tipster divulges inside information for his gain and your loss. The rhetorical pose of stockbrokers and racetrack tipsters to be offering prudent advice is contradicted by their circumstances, a contradiction catalogued in rhetoric as the "circumstantial ad hominem." That is to say, "Being so smart, why don't you do it yourself, if it's such good advice?"

"A tout," said Damon Runyon (1958 [1933], 19), who knew the score on the economics of prediction, "is a guy who goes around a race track giving out tips on the races, if he can find anybody who will listen to his tips, especially suckers, and a tout is nearly always broke. If he is not broke, he is by no means a tout, but a handicapper, and is respected by one and all." Runyon in truth was a sucker for tips himself, and lost so regularly and embarrassingly that he would buy a two-dollar ticket on every horse, to be able to exhibit a winner (Clark 1978, 197).

We know the force of the American Question and the Five-Hundred-Dollar-Bill Theorem as well as we know anything. If we know that the sun will rise tomorrow and that prime numbers are odd we know that people who were so smart would be rich and that sidewalks which were so filled with $500 bills would be cleared. Therefore a prediction about stocks—as distinct from mere current information about the market, a mere statement of the going odds, a mere consensus of public opinion, reflected in the price—is on average worthless.

It has been easy therefore to assemble statistical evidence that the Five-Hundred-Dollar-Bill Theorem is true about Wall Street:

stock markets everywhere do in fact jiggle about in unpredictable ways. The evidence is by now overwhelming. In 1933 Alfred Cowles, one of the founders of modern statistical economics, posed the question in a title, "Can Stock Market Forecasters Forecast?" He answered, "It is doubtful." Cowles himself had abandoned a forecasting business in 1931, ashamed of his failure to foresee the Great Crash. Burton Malkiel's *A Random Walk Down Wall Street* (1985) gives an accessible summary of the research since Cowles, such as P. H. Cootner, ed., *The Random Character of Stock Prices* (1964). The forecastability of stock prices continues to be at best doubtful.

It may be objected that sophisticated people do in fact buy stock market advice. An economist (and only an economist) would conclude that something of value had been bought. A reply has been suggested by James Burk, a sociologist and former stockbroker, who found that the advice-giving industry sprang from legal decisions early in the century (1988). The courts began to decide that the trustee of a pension fund or of a child's inheritance could be held liable for bad investing if he did not take advice. The effect would have been the same had the courts decided that prudent men should consult Ouija boards or the flights of birds. It was so at Rome: a consul who ignored the advice of the college of augurs was liable to prosecution after retirement. America decided through its judges that an industry giving advice on the stock market should come into existence, whether or not it was worthless. It did, and was. (Europe is not similarly blessed with an advice industry, because the law is different.) The industry can go out of existence the same way. The judge who first asks the American Question and rules a stockbroker liable for his unsuccessful advice will save many a widow and orphan from investment counseling.

It may be objected that after all a great deal of money is made in the stock market. But a great deal is also made at the track in Miami. Grandfather Stueland was offered Radio Corporation of America stock in the early 1920s and regretted later that he had invested in Stueland Electric instead. Some people did buy RCA: they must have known. But that some people win at the stock-broker or at the $100 window at Hialeah racetrack in lucky Miami does not mean that they were justified in their true belief. They could have won by luck rather than by a justifying technique. People win at slot machines, too, but cannot tell how, because they use no justifiable, inscribable, bookable technique. And even if some people *do* know they will win (God appears to them in a dream and tells them, maybe; or they have genuine inside know-ledge), there is no way for the common pigeon to know what these alleged experts know. Why would they be telling you, Bub?

It may be objected at last that the economist or other seer in the stock or bond or housing market does not have access to the big loans to make big money. Yet consortiums do have access to the big loans, and if the wisdom comes simply from being an econo-mist it ought to be simple to assemble a consortium of economists. A consortium of famous economists at Stanford and the Univer-sity of Chicago in the early 1970s believed that interest rates, which were then at shocking, unprecedented highs (6, 6.5, my Lord, even 7.5 percent), just had to come down. The price of bonds, in other words, just had to go up. A good time to buy bonds. The economists complained at lunch that their bankers would not loan them money to exploit this Sure Thing, The World's Greatest Secret. But in the event, sadly, the bankers were right. Interest rates did not fall; they rose. The consortium of econ-omists, relying on its collective expertise, lost its collective shirt.

The routine is the usual one. I myself have lost a shirt or two on real estate deals bound to succeed and on a consortium of econo-mists speculating in the foreign exchanges. From John Maynard Keynes (who lost money regularly before breakfast, but had a Cambridge College backing him up) and Irving Fisher (who re-duced Yale's endowment to half Harvard's by touting stocks in 1928) down to the latest scheme of some economist to make mon-ey from mathematical models of gold speculation, economists have not earned the confidence of bankers. As it was put by Paul

Samuelson, a student of these matters (1986 [1982], 541), "It's a mugs game for a dentist—or an associate professor of econometrics—to think that he and the telephone can have an edge over those who count the cocoa pods in Africa and follow the minute-by-minute arrival of new information."

The best known counterexample among economists is said to be the late Otto Eckstein, a fine economist with much common sense who extended the large-scale statistical model of the economy into commercial use. He built Data Resources, Inc. into a company with revenues in 1984 of $84 million. But Data Resources did not use its own predictions of prices and interest rates to speculate. It sold them to others, mainly to companies who wanted a myth of knowledge to comfort them in the world's uncertainty and to answer wrathful stockholders: "We took the best advice." If Data Resources had believed its own predictions to the extent of speculating on them, and was correct in its belief, then it could have become fabulously richer than it was. To say that Otto Eckstein or Paul Samuelson or other honest purveyors of economic tips became in fact a little bit rich does not answer the American Question. Eckstein and Samuelson (and Louis Rukeyser of Wall Street and Hot Horse Herbie of Broadway) became rich by *selling* advice, in the form of models and statistical equations and other charming talk, not by using it.

Cato the Elder reported of the haruspices, who examined livers in Rome with an expertise approaching the econometric, that they could not but laugh on meeting one another. Economists know lots of similar gags about their inability to predict profitably: forecasting is very difficult, especially if it is about the future; an economist is an expert who can tell you tomorrow why the thing he predicted yesterday didn't happen today; the best I can hope in a forecast is to be intelligently wrong or fortunately right.

One must not get carried away. Nobody doubts that a well-informed economist can tell you a thing or two about the future, mainly from knowing the present well. As the economist Robert Solow remarked about the predictions from Data Resources

(1982), "every month it provides an orderly description of the data, organized in such a way that one's attention is called to events that seem to conform with a reasonable person's understanding of the economy." The American Question casts no doubt on predictions that offer little or no profit. A prediction makes no profit if it is a commonplace or if does not offer a way to buy low and sell high. Predicting that the national income will not fall to zero next year is no more profitable than predicting that the sun will rise tomorrow.

Other people view economists as social weather forecasters. Economists are not so happy with the analogy, since they know they are not so smart. Weather forecasters and price forecasters could both earn a lot of money on a good forecast if they could keep it secret. In fact you will do better predicting a freeze in South Florida by watching the futures price of orange juice than by listening to the National Weather Service. Unsurprisingly, the growers and dealers have hired meteorologists to make predictions that are better than those of the Service.

Come to mention it, though, economists don't do much of a job as public forecasters. Victor Zarnowitz, the leading scholar in the field, makes only modest claims for the most promising method. A recent study by Zarnowitz and Geoffrey Moore (1982) showed that "leading indicators," invented by Moore and now reported monthly in the press, can indeed predict business cycle peaks— but with leads, alas, ranging from one to nineteen months. "The economists are generally right in their predictions," Sidney Webb said once, "but generally a good deal out in their dates." Predicting the end of prosperity as coming somewhere in the next nineteen months is a little better than saying that if it's August then Jamaica has fair chance after a while of getting a hurricane. Yet it is not so smart that the economic forecaster could retire to Jamaica. It is not good enough to be profitable; and if it were, it would be discounted already.

There are other ways of getting to the same doubt that economists can predict. For one thing, unlike humans, hurricanes are not listening. Humans react to economic predictions in ways that dampen or magnify the predictions. It would be as though the hurricane presently north of Jamaica reacted to a forecast that tomorrow it was going to move further away by saying "Hmm: I'd better turn around and go to Jamaica instead." This is the point made by the conservative economists who suggest that people have "rational expectations." One does not have to accept every part of such a theory to believe the more modest Theorem proposed here. It suggests modestly that people are not so stupid that they are easy to surprise. If they are not easy to surprise, then the economy is not easy to manipulate, and its would-be manipulators are not rich or powerful.

Further and more deeply the equations of fluid dynamics applicable to the weather do not include an equation that rules out cheap but profitable predictions. Economic models do. A person who was smart enough to know the solutions to the economic equations would be rich, unless profitable solutions were already anticipated and discounted by the model. But according to the Five-Hundred-Dollar-Bill Theorem they would already be discounted. If the alleged model is a widely available piece of information or if its essence were embodied in a widely held judgment, it would be useless for making anyone rich. Wise in retrospect, maybe; rich in prospect, no.

The American Question and the Five-Hundred-Dollar-Bill Theorem radically limit what economists and calculators can know about the future. No economist watches the TV program "Wall Street Week" without a vague sense that he is betraying his science. He should be pleased. His science proves its robustness by asserting confidently that the science cannot profitably predict; indeed, that no science of humankind can profitably predict, even the science of stockbrokers. The economic theorem is so powerful that it applies to economists.

The postmodern economist is modest about profitworthy detail, the detail from which she could buy low and sell high. She must be modest especially about the proud claim of economics in the 1960s, the claim to fine tune the economy, making detailed adjustments to money and taxes in order to offset a depression just around the corner. As economists and other expert knights of Camelot realize now after much tragedy sprung from hubris, if an economist could see around the corner she would be rich. Fine tuning violates the Theorem: a fine tuner would see dozens of $500 bills lying around her neighborhood. The knowledge that would make fine tuning possible would make the economists who have it fabulously wealthy. The economists go on relating impossibly detailed scenarios into the microphones of television reporters, but in their hearts they know they are wrong.

The American Question requires intellectual modesty in the economic expert, if he does not want people to laugh on meeting him. Hubris will need divine protection. Xenophon reported Socrates saying: "Those who intend to manage [*oikesein*] houses or cities well are in need of divination. For the craft of carpenter . . . or economics [*oikonomikon*] . . . may be learned . . . ; but the greatest of these matters the gods reserve to themselves. . . . If anyone supposes that these [divinations] are not beyond reason, and nothing in them beyond our judgment, he is himself beyond reason" (Xenophon, I.1.7). Socrates could turn to the oracles for divine supplementation of a craft. We have lost today the favor of the gods, and books on economic technique will not assuage our woe.

9   The Limits of Criticism

*I*f an economist were so smart, then, she would be rich. But there is more. The more leads back to the ancient and sensible doubt that critics can do as much in the way of art as artists can. The American Question mocks the hubris of the critic, whether the critic is a humanist or a scientist, a pundit or a policy-maker.

A crucial point is that the critic's coin of profit need not be monetary. Political power is there on the sidewalk, too, waiting to be picked up if there is something wrong with the 5,000-vote Theorem—that politicians and their advisors who think they see 5,000 votes sitting there waiting to be picked up are mistaken. But of course the Theorem is right. There does not exist a simple way, to be written down in a book, for getting 5,000 votes. The political scientists cannot predict elections in ways that would allow them to manipulate the outcome, doing better than the political artists they study.

Notice the clause of profitability. The political scientists can make predictions all right ("A declared revolutionary socialist will not soon be elected to the House of Representatives from Orange County"). But they cannot make valuable predictions ("Expenditure of $200,000 on ten-second spots on Channels 2, 7, and 9 during the three weeks before the election will assure the election of Jones to the House"). If two empires fight to the death a great empire will fall. The valuable and impossibly difficult prediction specifies which one.

This is not to say that $200,000 spent on television advertisements never won an election, or that after the election a political scientist could not interpret the events as a victory for money and television. And once it was a bright idea. After the advertisements won in the 5th Congressional District, however, it would become routine in the 4th and in the 6th and at length in the Nth. If it were so easy the 500-dollar or the 5,000-vote opportunity would be picked up. The supernormal profits, as economists put it, would be dissipated. The expected return from political advice, allowing for its uncertainty, should be approximately zero.

If a critic of elections is so smart then she should be able to sell the analysis. Isocrates the Sophist turned back the boast of the socratics that (unlike the sophists) they did not charge for their Truth. If your Truth is so valuable, why does it not meet a market test? A study of Political Action Committees that predicts elections on the basis of expenditure by the Committees should be sellable at least to the Committees. If not, perhaps it is not valuable advice. It may be good history, giving a sensible account of votes in the past, but it is apparently not good advice on how to add votes in the future. At the margin, as economists like to say, you get what you pay for. The American Question and the Five-Hundred-Dollar-Bill Theorem constrain all forward-looking arguments in the human sciences.

The payment need not be monetary, if money is not what the seer desires. Prestige in the local saloon would be cheaply available if the American Question did not also cast doubt on predictions of sporting events. But it does. The lineaments of the sporting future apparent to the average guy will be reflected in the sporting odds. Only fresh details give profits above average measured in money or prestige. Fresh details are hard to come by. Information, like steel and haircuts, is costly to produce.

The American Question can be asked of all predictions of trend, in journalism, sociology, political science, commercial art, and elsewhere. Some people can predict clothing fashions, for example, but not by a write-downable method. They may have a true belief, but in its justification it becomes false. If it can be made routine and written down it is no longer valuably true. Successful fashion designers have a private trick for which they are paid large sums and about which they are not anyway going to blab. If hem lengths followed the stock market (until recently of course they led it), then cheap fortunes could be made by exploiting the fact, and the fact would be exploited away. But cheap fortunes are oxymoronic.

As the man said about predictions on the stock market, it is doubtful that any prediction of tastes is possible. Predicting human tastes tends towards the oxymoronic, too. The claim that advertisers can predict and therefore manipulate tastes is good advertising for advertising, but otherwise doubtful. When Vance Packard wrote *The Hidden Persuaders,* which made frightening claims about the power of advertising, his friends in advertising were delighted. J. K. Galbraith likewise has done for Madison Avenue what it could not have done for itself, persuading influential people that advertisers have the power to make people buy their stuff. If tastes could be manipulated as easily as the critics of advertising say then the advertisers would be rich. It is not too surprising that a recent study at the University of Iowa has found that television advertising campaigns have less than their claimed power to change minds (Tellis 1988).

All manner of provision for the future is limited by the American Question. The legal rule of first possession, as in mining or inventing, for example, gives title to the coal seam or the patent to whoever gets there first, giving an incentive to waste resources in races such as the race between Kodak and Polaroid. The society would be better off if the outcome were properly anticipated by the sovereign power auctioning the entitlement off to the highest bidder. But as the legal economist David Haddock notes, "where new knowledge is at issue, finding appropriate solutions becomes more complex. In such situations, one cannot define an entitlement because one cannot imagine what one has not imagined" (1986, 789).

What is thrown into doubt by the American Question is a claim to systematic, justified, cheaply acquired, write-downable knowledge about profitable opportunities. The "profit," note again, is to be broadly construed. A small group of mathematicians has been complaining since early in the century that certain much-discussed mathematical objects cannot actually be constructed, even in principle. The late Errett Bishop, a leader of these "constructivists," used the American Question. A real least upper bound is supposed to exist for *every* bounded sequence (such as the bound that the sequence .9, .99, .999, .9999, .99999, . . . has at 1.0; but for *every* bounded sequence, however strange). The notion is used routinely in un-constructive, "formalist" analysis (which is most of modern mathematics). Bishop pointed out, however, that the bound would require for its construction, were it ever attempted, a systematic, write-downable "method M," applicable to all such sequences, even strange ones. But anyone so smart as to come up with method M would be mathematically rich: "Of course," wrote Bishop, "such a method M does not exist, and nobody expects that one will ever be found. Such a method would solve most of the famous unsolved problems in mathematics" (1985, 7). Like the ability to forecast interest rates or manipulate elections, method M is a five-hundred-dollar-bill machine, intellectually speaking.

The force of the American Question depends on the sums involved. A tiny edge on average over the stock market can make such a seer wealthy beyond the dreams of avarice. The sums extend beyond the normal return to normal education or normal effort. No one would deny that normal knowledge is worth its hire. So is special knowledge, when you can get it. But the special knowledge that the stockbroker or the economist or the tipster claims is not in fact special. It is easy to acquire, and therefore has no protection from entry, and therefore can earn no special return. Being able to read racing forms or study *Barron's* with care or run statistical fits on corn prices does not make one especially smart. Therefore, except by luck, one cannot get especially rich.

The American Question mocks the claims of predictors, social engineers, and critics of the social arts. The predictor who could get it usefully right would be a god incarnate, a diviner.

The reason is not that humans are too complicated or too changeable or too free. The humanistic criticisms of social science may be true but they are not telling; they are easy to make and easy to answer. The scientist answers, "Give us the money and we will finish the job." If humans are "ultimately" free considered as individuals, they still can be predicted on average and in the mass. And if human masses are complex they still can be predicted with another million dollars and another model. So long as humans are to be viewed as molecules bouncing against each other the problem is merely to get the mathematics right. It is said that predicting human beings is bound to be more complicated than predicting planets or pigeons, but that is not true. It depends on what you are trying to predict. The daily temperature variation of a human is easier to predict than the twitching of the sixty-seventh feather from the pigeon's tail. It is a matter of how ambitious the prediction is. The "simple" problem of space flight, "merely" an application of Newton's laws, requires days of computation at high speed if the ambition is to put a rocket precisely *there* on Mars. For a given ambition the complexity is only a matter of computer time.

The American Question puts more fundamental limits on what we humans can say about ourselves. It puts a limit on mechanical models of human behavior. It does not make the mechanical models useless for interesting history or routine prediction; it just makes them useless for gaining an edge about the future. If people were as predictable as naive behaviorism alleges, for instance, the psychologists would be rich and the personnel managers all-powerful. The field of industrial and managerial psychology was erected in the 1930s on just such a putative Secret, but led to miracles only on 34th Street (Waring, forthcoming). To recur to economics, the various "solutions" of bargaining problems have this flaw: that if the economist knew the solution, then so would the players, which would make the solution valueless. The computer that could predict the next move of a competitor would sell for a lot of money. If computers are cheap, no one can get rich by using them to outsmart others.

Likewise there are limits on the teachability of skills. It is paradoxical to claim that a Ph.D. qualifies one to teach "entrepreneurship," or even "excellence." The present content of the American business school, with its burden of mechanical technique, undervalues the stories and moralities that make a business culture. In pure form the successful person of business is either a lucky fool or a godlike genius. It is hard to tell the difference. I have a friend who is a businessman with spectacular recent successes, earning enormous amounts for his company, a big one. Not being a fool in any sense he looks with foreboding on what will happen to his reputation for genius when the coin turns up tails, as with 50-50 probability it will. Perhaps he understates his genius, for there *is* a genius about the entrepreneur, by which the pursuit of his own interest promotes a good social end which was no part of his intention.

It can be argued that capitalism depends for its progressiveness on such geniuses. It is observationally equivalent to say that it depends on large numbers of fools, mucking about in garages and board rooms, some of whom will be lucky (Nye 1989). A colleague in the English Department at the University of Iowa, Donald Marshall, put it this way in a note to me: "what motivates economic activity is the delusion that we can guess the future, and expertise is deployed, unbeknownst to itself, to protect us from discovering that in fact we can't do so, a discovery that would lead us to despair and paralysis. The joke is that . . . capitalism's advantage is that it maximizes the number of people who have this delusion." The clerkly treason against capitalism is contemptible, since capitalism supports the clerks. Yet there are enough rich and lucky fools to give point to the clerk's report: If you're so rich why aren't you smart?

Take publishing. Experts cannot use routine methods to improve on the tacit knowledge of a publisher. This is not an excuse for a publisher to ignore formal methods such as computerized inventory systems. It says merely that formal methods will not earn abnormally high profits for long. The formality makes them easy to copy. Going to business school is not a way to acquire immense wealth, because it is too easy to get in. The $500 bills get snapped up. The tacit and informal character of what is left for human decisions is why the publishers get paid for taking the blame. No artificial intelligence could have predicted the success of Hofstadter's *Gödel, Escher, Bach;* no central planner that of *Animal Farm.* In fact the publishers themselves did not predict it. Entrepreneurs seek and sometimes find, given proper license to stumble. One of the many American publishers who turned down *Animal Farm* explained that they weren't doing animal stories that year.

The humanities cannot be taught by machine, either. Gary Walton, an economist and former dean of a business school, has written a book called *Beyond Winning* about "philosopher coaches," such as Woody Hayes in football or John Wooden in basketball. He is aware that if coaching could be learned from a book the woods would be full of Woodys and Woodens. If coaching were mechanical in its effects on the athletes then East Germany would never lose an Olympic contest. The ability to teach exceptional performance is itself an exceptional performance. What can be said about the athletic case is what can be said about the scholarly case: that a great coach or a great scholar teaches not by instructing the students in a bookable technique but by exhibiting a way of life, which not all can follow.

The limit on calculability and sayability applies to language and rhetoric itself. If anyone could get what they wished by shouting, for example, then everyone would shout, as at a cocktail party, arriving by the end hoarse but without having gotten what they wished. H. P. Grice affixed an economic tag to the trumping of speech conventions, "exploitation." As Stephen Levinson put the point in his book *Pragmatics,*

There is a fundamental way in which a full account of the communicative power of language can never be reduced to a set of conventions for the use of language. The reason is that wherever some convention or expectation about the use of language arises, there will also therewith arise the possibility of the non-conventional *exploitation* of that convention or expectation. It follows that a purely conventional or rule-based account of natural language usage can never be complete (1983, 112; italics added)

A rhetorical analysis has this limit, that it can tell wisely and well how a speech has gone in the past, but cannot be expected to provide The World's Greatest Secret for the future. It can show how Cicero in *Pro Archia* exploited tricolon, how Descartes exploited rhetoric to attack rhetoric itself, or how Jane Austen in *Northanger Abbey* exploited an irony that was always intended, covert, finite, and stable. But rhetoric cannot be finished and formulaic, or else anyone could be a Cicero, Descartes, or Austen. The chimera of a once-finished formula for language must be left to Fregean philosophy or to magic.

In the opening lines of *Faust*, before the Doctor has turned in vexation to magic, he laments that "I see that we can know nothing! / It nearly breaks my heart." He immediately amends this sweeping skepticism, for the American Question does not imply literally that we can know nothing but merely, as he then complains on behalf of his fellow men, that he can know nothing *to better Mankind*, as he puts it. On further reflection he comes to the nub: his studies, damn them, have taught him nothing that betters *Herr Dr. Faust*, this very example of Mankind. "And *I* have neither property nor money, / Nor honor and glory in the world: / No dog should go on living so." There lies the tragedy, at the impossibility of predictions profitable to Faust himself. He seeks The World's Greatest Secret for personal profit; which in due course he obtains, though not for free on the sidewalk, and then gets his fill of property and money.

Lacking the Devil's bargain, science cannot predict itself. The paradox shows up in economics because economics so plainly must apply to itself, if it's so smart. But the paradox applies to any foreknowledge of new knowledge. The impossibility of self-prediction has become a commonplace in philosophy. You do not know today what you will decide tomorrow, unless you have already decided it, in which case it is not tomorrow but today that you decide it.

"Prescience" is an oxymoron, like cheap fortunes: pre-science, knowing before one knows. Prescience is required for central planning of science. The philosophers Karl Popper and Alasdair MacIntyre among others have pointed out that knowing the future of science requires knowing the science of the future. It is not to be done. MacIntyre notes that the unpredictability of mathematical innovation is a rigorous case, resting on theorems concerning the incompleteness of arithmetic and the incalculability of certain expressions, proven by Gödel and Church in the 1930s. And "if the future of mathematics is unpredictable, so is a great deal else" (MacIntyre 1981, 90). If someone claims to know what method or lack of method would yield good science, why isn't he scientifically rich?

The other arts are similarly constrained. Some critics in the eighteenth century believed they had methods for assuring excellence in drama or painting. Nowadays no one would claim to have a formulaic, bookable method for constructing excellent paintings, except as a postmodern joke. The method would solve painting, in the sense that tic-tac-toe has been solved. This is not to say that rules of perspective or color harmonies cannot be constructed and applied. They can, the way a poet can check for agreement with the meter she has chosen or a dancer can check his fifth position. It says only that there is at present no routine, book-readable method for achieving artistic riches. The unusually profitable opportunities have been picked up, leaving only the routine returns to routine ability.

Each bit of the accumulated routine was once someone's personal and profitable trick. The genius has more tricks than the rest of us, which become tomorrow's routines. The first Florentine businessman to use double-entry bookkeeping gained a control over his materials similar in value to the first Athenian sculptor to use the slouch of standing bodies. In this age of iron, however, no one earns $500 from the mere idea of double entries or contrapposto. And the point is that any present day is an age of iron, because gold is picked up as soon as it appears.

The distinction between routine predictions and startling and profitable divination is analogous to the distinction between routine cooking and the profitable Art of three-star cookery. In his peculiar little dialogue, the *Ion,* Plato/Socrates lampoons Ion the performing Artist who imagines he *knows* something. It is significant that to mock Ion's claim to knowledge Socrates uses the example of divining. Allan Bloom once remarked of the passage:

If divining is to be considered an art, it is strange in that it must profess to know the intentions of the gods; as an art, it would, in a sense, seem to presuppose that the free, elusive gods are shackled down by the bonds of intelligible necessity. Divining partakes of the rational dignity of the arts while supposing a world ruled by divine beings who are beyond the grasp of the arts. (1970, 57)

As Plato and the American Question would say, the claim of divining to be an art, Greek *techne,* mere bookable craft, is absurd.

Plato therefore wished to cage poetry, the god-possession that flatters men to think they know more than does the honest artisan, a technician in every sense. The followers of Plato down to the age of technique are enamored of knowledge as *techne,* a craft written down in books. They propose to cast books lacking such craft into the flames, as poetry and pretense, mere sophistry and illusion. The trouble is that their version of the fully rational life, the bookable final rules for language games, requires non-routine prediction. And in human affairs a prediction beyond what earns routine returns is impossible, except by entrepreneurs, idiot savants, *auteurs,* and other prodigies of tacit knowledge. The notion that bookable knowledge can guide the world through its difficult moments, like the notion that central planning can guide an economy, is self-contradictory. If the philosopher kings and central planners were so smart they would be rich.

As indeed they are, for a reason other than their ability to predict. They live in a world every hopeful that procedure, mechanism, calculation, bureaucracy, MBA degrees, and other social *techne* will keep us warm and safe. It will not, as the American

Question reminds us so sharply, though the world is willing to pay for the illusion.

This is not to say that the project of getting knowledge about the economy or about poems and paintings is worthless. Inside the margin, as economists say, it is worthful. The world runs on little else. Everyone needs to know how to write with an alphabet, though it took a Phoenician genius to think it up and make his fortune. No one afterwards, though, can expect to make a fortune by knowing the ABCs.

An economist looking at the business world is like a critic looking at the art world. Economists and other human scientists can reflect intelligently on present conditions and can tell useful stories about the past. These produce wisdom, which permits broad, conditional "predictions." Some are obvious; some require an economist; but none is a machine for achieving fame or riches.

The economist says: if a government puts a tax on property the people whose property is made more valuable by good schools will in fact pay for the schools. Or again: if voluntary restrictions on Japanese automobile imports are retained then the Japanese manufacturers will benefit by about $1,000 per car and the American auto buyers will pay about $160,000 per year for each job saved in Detroit. Though useful as wisdom, and justifying the economist's role as critical theorist, neither of these predictions is bankable.

The argument is merely that at the margin, where supernormal profits and reputations for genius are being made, the observer's knowledge is not the same as the doer's, the critic is no improvement as artist over the artist, the model of the future is no substitute for the entrepreneur's god-possessed hunch. The critics become ridiculous only when they confuse speaking well about the past with doing well in the future. Critics of art and literature stopped being ridiculous this way a long time ago. It would be good if critics of society would join them in their modest sophistication.

To become an effective manager or college dean the consistent modernist must unlearn his modernism—the notion that Procedure will tell all. If it were easy to organize "correctly," then people would do it, which is what is wrong with the journalistic notion that it is easy for business to choose the Swedish Way or the Japanese Way or whatever Way is currently on their minds. The hubris of social engineering is the same as the hubris of facile social criticism.

No one is justly subject to the American Question who retains a proper modesty about what observation and recording and storytelling can do. We can observe the history of economies or the history of painting, and in retrospect tell a story about how security of commercial property or the analysis of vanishing points made for good things. An expert such as an economist is an expert on the past, and about the future that can be known without divine and profitable possession. Human scientists and critics of human arts, in other words, write history, not prophecy.

*H*arry Truman had it about right. The expert as expert, a bookish sort consulting what is already known, cannot by his nature learn anything new, because then he wouldn't be an expert. He would be an entrepreneur, a statesman, or an Artist with a capital A. The expert critic can make these non-expert entrepreneurs more wise, perhaps, by telling them about the past. But he must settle for low wages. Smartness of the expert's sort cannot proceed to riches.

Economics teaches this. What it teaches is the limit on social engineering. It teaches that we can be wise and good but not foresighted in detail. Economics has something to teach the humanities, if they happen to think they know the future of art. It has a lot to teach experts, if they believe in magic.

10   Keeping the Company of Economists

*It is now sixteen or seventeen years since I saw the
Queen of France, then the Dauphiness, at Versailles. . . .
Little did I dream that I should have lived to see disasters
fallen upon her in a nation of gallant men. . . . I thought ten
thousand swords must have leaped from their scabbards
to avenge even a look that threatened her with insult.
But the age of chivalry is gone. That of sophisters,
economists, and calculators, has succeeded; and the glory
of Europe is extinguished for ever.*

Edmund Burke, *Reflections on the Revolution
in France,* Everyman ed., p. 73.

*T*he experts claim that their stories are "positive, not norma-
tive," "is" instead of "ought," the way things are as against how
they should be. The claim is at the center of modernism. But stories
carry an ethical burden. Concealing the ethical burden under a
cloak of science is the master move of expertise, the secret ingre-
dient of the snake oil.

Adam Smith was a professor of moral philosophy. John Stuart
Mill was a moral and political philosopher. Since then the stories
of the worldly philosophers have seemed to drift away from ethics.
But the subject of economics is ethical, which makes a claim to
sidestep ethics worrisome. We do not worry over much if an astro-
physicist refuses to think ethically about his stories. We should if
an economist refuses.

The literary critic Kurt Heinzelman has placed this "divorcing
[of] philosophy from economics" in the emblematic year of 1871,
when John Stuart Mill issued his last edition of *Principles of Political Economy* and William Stanley Jevons, the new scientist of
economics, published *The Theory of Political Economics* (Heinzelman 1980, 85–87). By 1900 the *Dictionary of Political*

Economy could formulate the business of economics in a way that few economists would now dispute:

> The relation of morals to economics is often misunderstood. Political economy is, properly speaking, a science rather than an art. [Note the English use of "science."] It aims in the first instance at the explanation of a certain class of facts. . . . The special knowledge of economic facts possessed by the economist may enable him to give valuable advice on economic questions, but this, strictly speaking, is not his business. His business is to explain, not to exhort. It is therefore beside the mark to speak of economists, as such, preaching a low morality or rejecting morality altogether. (Montague 1900)

The economist was to be seen as a man of business, not a preacher. He sold Gradgrind facts, not the mere preaching of morality. In 1900 the word "preach" already sneered, as teenagers now sneer at their parents' preaching. The *Dictionary* claims too that the economic facts are science rather than art. By 1900 the specialization of "science" in English to mean "lab-coated and quantitative" was accomplished already. The peculiarly English definition made it easy for Jevons and other English-speaking economists this century past to suppose that a science could have nothing to do with morality.

It would be a strange economics, of course, that did not treat at least the pursuit of happiness, and therefore the morality of getting more. Economics has a branch called "welfare economics" into which moral questions have been diverted since the 1920s. The graduate schools teach that the sole moral judgment an economist should make is the least controversial one: if every person is made better off by some change, the change (being "Pareto optimal") should take place. Even philosophers like John Rawls have adopted the notion of Pareto optimality, trying in the economist's manner to pull a decently detailed moral theory out of a hat. Welfare economics has shown recently some stirrings of more complex moral life, as in the works of the economist and philosopher Amartya Sen. But mainly welfare economics is Victorian utilitarianism stuffed and mounted and fitted with marble eyes.

The demise of moral reasoning in the late nineteenth century and early twentieth century would not come as news to Wayne Booth of the University of Chicago, the very model of a modern major professor, who wrote in 1988 a book called *The Company We Keep: An Ethics of Fiction*. He begins by noting how thoroughly since modernism the students of literature have segregated off the moral questions. "There is no such thing as a moral or an immoral book," said Oscar Wilde. "Books are well written or badly written. That is all." As was his talent, Wilde spoke only a little before his time. Biologists, historians, economists, even the theologians of the age subscribed at last to this bit of modernist amorality. There is no such thing as a moral or an immoral economy. Economies are efficient or inefficient. That is all. In this life "we want nothing but Facts, sir; nothing but Facts!"

Booth's book gives a reply. It suggests to an economist that the "ethical criticism" it propounds can reach beyond literature. Booth himself takes ethical criticism as far as the Ajax Kitchen Cleanser jingle. It can be taken all the way to economics and its unconscious use of ethics-laden stories. Tzvetan Todorov put the matter so: "literature . . . is a discourse oriented towards—let us not be intimidated by the ponderous words—truth and morality. . . . If we have managed to lose sight of that essential dimension of literature, it is because we began by reducing truth to verification and morality to moralism" (1987 [1984], 164). For "literature" read "economics."

The easiest point is that economists have ethics, perforce. Booth remarks that "even those critics [he could have said economists] who work hard to purge themselves of all but the most abstract formal interests turn out to have an ethical program in mind" (1988, 7). All right: ideology motivates economists, despite their protestations of ideological innocence.

The big point, however, is not ideology and its inability to see itself. We know that already. The big point is that economic stories, as Booth argues in detail for novelists, have an ethical burden: "We all live a great proportion of our lives in a surrender to stories. . . . Even the statisticians and accountants must *in fact* conduct their daily business largely in stories: the reports they give to superiors; the accounts they deliver to tax lawyers; the anecdotes and parables they hear." (Booth 1988, 14, italics his). "All of us spontaneously make narratives out of just about every bit of information that comes our way" (162). "It is impossible to shut our eyes and retreat to a story-free world" (236). If we enter into it we "embrace the patterns of desire of any narrative" (285).

Start the ethical criticism of economics, then, with Booth's central question about the corruptions of literature (11): "What kind of company are we keeping as we read or listen?" As our mothers told us, keeping bad or good company is bad for us or good. Though he can hardly be faulted for not reflecting on academic life in other books, Wayne Booth does not in *The Company We Keep* examine the reading and listening to science and scholarship (as against literature), and the company therefore that teachers and scholars keep.

The levels at which we are asked to be a kind of person by economic writing need to be distinguished.

First, the scientific paper in economics has an implied reader it shares with other self-consciously scientific productions of the culture. The implied reader has some features that are unattractive: he is cold-blooded, desiccated, uninvolved. The case of Isaac Newton and his invention, the scientific paper, is the model (Bazerman 1988, chap. 4).

Along with high-minded precepts about the production of science the scientific paper encourages the low-minded notion that other moral questions are "just matters of opinion." The scientific paper in economics treats ethical matters of income distribution, for example, as unarguable, like one's preference for chocolate ice cream. The question that remains of course, is, "How do we think about our judgments, once we decide that our goal is to *think* about them and not simply to assert them?" (Booth 1988, 59). The values asserted by the scientific paper in economics and elsewhere are certainly not all bad. But it is worth remarking sharply that they are not all good, either, even though scientific.

Second point about the people we are asked to be in the reading of economic texts is more particularly economic. The economist asks the reader to take on certain ethical positions for the sake of the economistic argument. Most of us don't like the implied reader of economic stories: "Am I willing to be the kind of person that this storyteller is asking me to be?" (33). About the coldly calculating *homo economicus,* no, say we: "A levelling, rancorous, rational sort of mind / That never looked out of the eye of a saint / Or out of a drunkard's eye." And yet the cold calculation had better be done, by someone, or else we will bomb civilians at night for no gain or choose manned space flight over unmanned. The person you are asked to be in a modern economic argument is not entirely attractive, but is not a character that society can do without. He is usefully realistic about constraints and choices, though a little unreflective.

On utilitarian grounds, in other words, the economist is necessary. In policy questions the ethical position that economics recommends is that of the social engineer, who provides plans indifferently for full employment or extermination camps. The social engineer will protest that he would have nothing to do with extermination camps. But then he must ask where he draws the line, an ethical deliberation that economists are reluctant to undertake.

Third, as Booth says, "artists often imitate the roles they create. The writer is moved, in reality, toward the virtues or vices imagined for the sake of the work itself" (108). The same is true of academics, perhaps more so. Historians of the medieval papacy or students of comparative politics adopt their subjects' methods, at least in spirit. It is not irrelevant that Henry Kissinger's first book was on Metternich. Anthropologists have begun to wonder recently about the effects their people have on them. About time.

For economics the analysis of the ethical effects of the roles they create is simple, and partly true. Some economists imitate the role of *ipse homo economicus* they have created (compare Klamer 1983). Anyone who has administered economists will report that a third or so of them behave in selfish ways, justifying their behavior when challenged by smirking reference to the economic model of man. "If I serve on the search committee I want a more than an average raise next year." "Jim, you're kidding: I can't hitch salary to routine service in such a mechanical way. We're in this together." "Ha! Don't talk to me about togetherness. You believe in economics, don't you?" Historians and doubtless professors of literature have their own occupational diseases, but cheeky selfishness is not one of them. It's not done in their circles; it is in economics, because of the market stories the economists tell. For the same reason it would be impossible to get a group of modern economists in academic life or the government to vote themselves strictly equal salary increases, so deeply do they believe in the ethics of competition. The egalitarian solution regularly occurs in university departments of history, some of which in fact vote on salaries.

The ethical effect of paying close attention to economic behavior, to repeat, is not entirely bad. Economists suggest sometimes that the splendid rationality they study is worthy of imitation. Economics provides the rudiments of ethical thinking for a bourgeois age: accumulate; think ahead; be methodical if it suits the task; be as honest as is the local custom; above all, do not feel socially inferior to an impulsive aristocracy—their day is done. The point is that the ethical thinking of the bourgeoisie is not worthless (an economist would make reflexively the joke that after all it has sold well). Most of those who sneer at it are the beneficiaries of its virtues, which, "during its rule of scarce one hundred [now near 250] years has created more massive and more colossal forces than have all preceding generations together." And since Marx and Engels penned these lines in their *Manifesto* the real income per head of Americans has increased by a factor of ten and of late comers to capitalism by more. Viewed socially, the economic man is no pest.

Even viewed from a strictly individual point of view the merchant's virtues, though not those of Achilles or Jesus, are not ethical zeroes. In his wretched play at the dawn of bourgeois power (1731), George Lillo has his priggish ideal of the London merchant, Thorowgood, assert that "as the name of merchant never degrades the gentleman, so by no means does it exclude him" (1952 [1731], 294). Lillo lays it on thick. In the same scene Thorowgood on exiting instructs his assistant to "look carefully over the files to see whether there are any tradesmen's bills unpaid." One can smile from an aristocratic height at the goody-goody leanings of bourgeois ethics. But after all, in seriousness, it is not a matter of ethics to pay one's tailor? What kind of person accepts the wares of tradesmen and then refuses to give something in return? No merchant he.

The honesty of a society of merchants in fact goes beyond what would be strictly self-interested in a society of rats, as one can see in that much-maligned model of the mercantile society, the small Midwestern city. A reputation for fair dealing is necessary for a roofer whose trade is limited to a city of 50,000. One bad roof and he is ruined. A professor at the University of Iowa refused to tell at a cocktail part the name of a roofer in Iowa City who had at first done a bad job (he redid the job free, at his own instigation) because the roofer would be finished in town if his name got out. The professor's behavior itself shows that ethical habits of selfish origin can harden into ethical convictions, the way a child grows from fear of punishment towards servicing an internal master. A rat would have told the name of the roofer, to improve the story. After all, the professor's own reputation in business was not at stake.

The economist who relishes the telling of a story of greed is advocating it, whatever he may say about "is" and "ought." Certainly since the beginning of modern economics the economist has urged us to look on the good side of greed. Again: The morality of the almighty dollar is not the worst of moralities. Dr. Johnson said, "There are few ways in which a man can be more innocently employed than in getting money." "The more one thinks of this, [said

Strahan] the juster it will appear" (Boswell 1949 [1791], 532; 27 March 1775). So it has appeared in the long conversation after 1775. The economists have been arguing since the eighteenth century that the ancient and aristocratic distaste for acquisitiveness is naive ethically. It is naive because it fails to see that greed prospers in a market economy only by satisfying the ultimate consumers.

Donald Trump offends. But for all the jealous criticism he has provoked he is not a thief. He did not get his billions from aristocratic cattle raids, acclaimed in bardic glory. He made, as he put it, deals. All of them voluntary. He did not use a .38 or a broadsword to get people to agree. He bought the Commodore Hotel low and sold it high because Penn Central, Hyatt Hotels, and the New York City Board of Estimate—and behind them the voters and hotel guests—put the old place at a low value and the new place, trumped up, at a high value. Trump earned a suitably fat profit for seeing that a hotel in a low-value use could be moved into a high-value use. An omniscient central planner would have ordered the same move. Market capitalism can be seen as the most altruistic of systems, each capitalist working to help, for pay. Trump does well by doing good.

And yet there is an ethical problem in the theory and practice of economics. The problem is deeper than the mere distaste for calculation of selfishness or greed. Booth argues persuasively that a good author is a good friend, the good friend being "a kind of company that is not only pleasant or profitable, in some immediate way, but also good for me, good for its own sake. . . . Hours spent with this best kind of friend are seen as the way life should be lived. . . . My true friend is one who [quoting Aristotle] 'has the same relations with me that he has with himself' " (1988, 146–47).

The model of economics conserves on this sort of friendship, trying to get along on as little of its as possible. Economics was once described as the science of conserving love. The notion is that love is scarce, and that consequently we had better try to get along without it, organizing our affairs to take advantage of the abundant selfishness instead. The argument is economic to the core. As Adam Smith said famously, "It is not from the benevolence of the butcher, the brewer, or the baker, that we expect our dinner, but from their regard to their own interest" (1976 [1776], 16).

Smith did not overlook love—on the contrary, he wrote what he himself thought was his best book on *The Theory of Moral Sentiments*. Yet he never worked out the connection between his theory of love and his theory of selfishness. The problem is that conserving on love, treating it as terrifically scarce, and not expecting it, may be a bad way to encourage its growth. That is the modern social democratic position against market capitalism—that market capitalism discourages love (massive government bureaucracies, say the social democrats, encourage it).

The novelists did better in thinking about love and selfishness. It has long been realized that not economists but novelists first gave prominence to commercial selfishness. Novelists, poets, and playwrights, not primarily social theorists, were the first to portray the bourgeoisie. Smith's *Wealth of Nations* was just described as a "theory of selfishness." That is the reading that a modern economist gives the book, projecting back onto the father the sins of the children. In truth the book itself does not support such a reading very well. Smith never describes a project of rational selfishness without noting the emotional and moral obstacles to achieving it. Foreign trade free of tariffs, for example, is recommended by more than "police" (that is to say, policy, expediency, the achieving of high incomes). Most fundamentally, free trade accords with natural rights.

Notably, the idea of *homo economicus* comes late to economics, towards the end of the nineteenth century, by way of an analogy with physical molecules. Yet it comes early to the English novel, full blown in Defoe circa 1720, or prominent later in, say, Austen's comedies of calculation circa 1800 or Dickens' satires of acquisitiveness circa 1840.

Homo economicus is a facer of choices, a spurner of options known in the trade as "opportunity costs." The notion of opportunity cost, central to modern economics, does not become clear to economists until the Austrian economists of the 1870s. Yet it has ever been a commonplace of poets, two roads diverging in a yellow wood, and I, being one traveler, able to take only one. The road not taken is the opportunity cost. So is Achilles' road of fighting not taken to sulk in his tent or Satan's road of serving in Heav'n not taken to reign in Hell.

Look at Robinson Crusoe selecting what to load on his first raft trip from the wreck:

It was in vain to sit still and wish for what was not to be had, and this Extremity rouz'd my Application. . . . Hope of furnishing my self with Necessaries, encourag'd me to go beyond what I should have been able to have done upon another Occasion. My raft was now strong enough to bear any reasonable Weight; my next Care was what to load it with. . . . Having considered well what I most wanted, I first got three of the Seamen's Chests . . . and lowered them down. . . . The first of these I filled with Provision, *viz.* Bread, Rice, three Dutch Cheeses. . . . This put me upon rummaging for Clothes, . . . but [I] took no more than I wanted for present use, for I had other things which my Eye was more upon, as first Tools to work with on Shore, and it was after long searching that I found out the Carpenter's Chest, . . . much more valuable than a Ship Loading of Gold. . . . My next Care was for some Ammunition and Arms. (1975 [1719], 41–42)

This is a commercial man having to make choices under conditions of "scarcity" (another notion articulated late in economics, well after the novelists had shown it working in their stories). The raft is not of infinite size; at any moment the weather may turn and sink the wreck; this may be Crusoe's only trip. He cannot have everything, and so must make choices. He takes only the clothing he "wanted for present use," because there were "other things which my eye was more upon." That is, he chose to have fewer clothes and more carpenter's tools. He could not in the circumstances have both. He faced a road of many clothes or a diverging one of many tools and had to choose between them. He later "resolv'd to set all other Things apart [the opportunity costs], 'till I got every Thing out of the Ship that I could get" (44).

Each time Crusoe or any *homo economicus* faces a choice he draws up a balance sheet in his head—Crusoe speaks in the passage just cited of calling "a Council, that is to say, in my Thoughts, whether I should take back the Raft," but more commonly he uses commercial metaphors, especially those of accounting (most particularly on pp. 53–54). This is the rational way to proceed—understanding the word "rational" to mean merely the sensible adjustment of what you can do to what you want. So the rational person is a calculator, like Crusoe, making rough and ready choices about what to put next on the boat. After the second storm destroys the wreck, "I . . . recover'd my self with this satisfactory Reflection, *viz.* That I had lost no time, nor abated no Diligence to get everything out of her that could be useful to me" (47).

The details of the style throughout the book contribute to the force of scarcity—a contrast to the stories of shipwrecks in the *Odyssey* or the *Aeneid,* over which hover intervening gods willing to perform miracles of abundance. The miracles in Crusoe's world are naturalistic, reflecting always Adam's Curse in a way we have come to call "realistic." Defoe's story is filled with realistic disappointments, signalled often by an ominous "but." "There had been some Barly and Wheat together" on the wreck, "*but,* to my great Disappointment, I found afterwards that the Rats had eaten or spoil'd it all" (41). The wreck had "a great Roll of Sheet Lead: *But* this last was so heavy, I could not hoise [sic] it up to get it over the Ship's Side" (45). He takes a kid from a she-goat, and "hopes to have bred it up tame, *but* it would not eat, so I was forc'd to kill it and eat it myself" (50). He endeavored to breed some young wild pigeons, "*but* when they grew older they flew all away" (62). "May 4. I went a fishing, *but* caught not one Fish that I durst eat of" (68). "I searched for a *Cassava* root, . . . *but* I could find none" (79). He spent three days bringing grapes to his cave, "*But,* before I got thither, the Grapes were spoil'd" (80). The "but" is realistic, unsentimental, aware of life's scarcity. It is the economist's favorite conjunction.

Crusoe makes choices between goods, a workaday choice, not

between good and evil. The absurdity is not making a choice, like Burridan's ass, starving because he could not choose between two equally delicious piles of hay. *Homo economicus* may or may not be bad company for us, but literary artists, not the worldly philosophers, are responsible for getting us acquainted.

If economists tell stories and exercise an ethical sense when telling them, then they had better have as many stories as possible. This is a principled justification of pluralism, an argument for not keeping all one's eggs in a single narrative basket. If you are accustomed to thinking in Platonic terms within which knowledge consists mainly of propositions like the irrationality of the square root of two, provable now and forever, then monism looks attractive. There's One Truth out there, isn't there? If you are by contrast accustomed to thinking in Aristotelian terms within which knowledge consists of judgments like the desirability of democracy, uncertain even when agreed to after much discussion by people of good will, then monism in the tales we tell looks foolish, as it is.

"Powerful narrative," writes Booth, "provides our best criticism of other powerful narratives" (1988, 237). Maybe. Powerful metaphors do the job, too. But there is no doubt that the mutual criticism of the rhetorical tetrad is what's called for. The application to economics is straightforward. A variety in economic narratives is good for the soul. Marxist narrative provides a criticism of the bourgeois "neoclassical" narrative, and vice versa. "The serious ethical disasters produced by narratives occur when people sink themselves into an unrelieved hot bath of one kind of narrative" (237). Dogmatic Marxists, dogmatic neoclassicals, dogmatic Austrian economists, dogmatic institutionalists, who have put the other's writings on an index of forbidden books, are ethically dangerous, all of them. They are true believers, or, rather, believers in Truth. The best lack all conviction, while the worst / Are full of passionate intensity.

The Boothian pluralism of stories, then, speaks to economics. Albert Jonsen and Stephen Toulmin have recently noted the failures of "principled dogmatism," the one-story world, as an approach to morality—"legalism without equity, and moralism without charity" (1988, 342). Economics is a spur to such dogmatism, attempting to reduce ethical questions to a system of axioms. The stories of economists could better be used casuistically, as Jonsen and Toulmin would urge. The case-by-case method is quite opposed to modernism, and was attacked by Pascal in his *Provincial Letters* of 1656–57 on modernist grounds (Jonsen and Toulmin 1988, chap. 12). It does not seek universal principles to be applied by social engineers. It seeks an ethical conversation in which principles of less-than-universal applicability are discovered.

The best economists do exactly this. Ronald Coase, for example, is a British-educated economist for a long time on the faculty of the Law School of the University of Chicago. His approach to economics is casuistic, looking for the stories and metaphors and facts and logics that fit the case at hand, and avoiding the unreasonable obsession with one of them alone. His most famous article, "The Problem of Social Cost" (1988 [1960]), is exactly casuistic. It has therefore been misunderstood by modernist economists, who see in it a "theorem" for their social engineering. The theorem, as it happens, is due to Adam Smith, some years in advance of Coase (namely, that exchange free of trammels works well; Coase's point was the opposite, that in a world of trammels the particular trammels need to be examined one by one to decide about things like air pollution and property rights). A style of ethical storytelling that insists that cases matter as much as principles is foreign to most of modern economics.

The application of an ethics of fiction to economics, though, can hardly fail to teach also in the other direction. Students of literature can learn a thing or two about ethics from economists, and not only the ethical points already sketched—that bourgeois values have their value and that we must be grown-ups and face scarcity when after all it exists. The additional lesson in ethics that literary people can take from economics—economics of any sort, and indeed from social science of any sort—is that action is social. Booth takes ethical matters to be one-on-one affairs. An economist listening to the stories told by Adam Smith, David Ricardo, Knut Wicksell, John Maynard Keynes, or Paul Samuelson cannot narrow the ethical question down to me and thee. The economist has too lively an appreciation of the we. An economically consequential book—from *Atlas Shrugged* to *The General Theory of Employment, Interest and Money*—can have its consequences in wholly unintended ways on the individual reader (which Booth emphasizes) and in wholly unintended ways on people beyond the reader (which he does not). For example, *Atlas Shrugged* can inadvertently sustain a country-club Republicanism far removed from the romance of the novel. *The General Theory* can help create an atmosphere of democratic interventionism that results in a permanent underclass of welfare recipients serviced by well-paid bureaucrats.

In other words, the economist looks for moral consequences beyond the dyad of author and reader. A book can have obviously good ethical effects on individuals, encouraging them to save (to take the standard Keynesian example), yet the saving can have bad effects in the society at large. We recognize the pursuit of profit as an ethical failing in an individual—relative to Pauline perfection, at least—yet at the social level it can lead to good.

The classic definition of economics was given by Alfred Marshall in 1890 on the first page of his *Principles of Economics*— "a study of mankind in the ordinary business of life." To this the literary critic Northrop Frye would answer, "The fundamental job of the imagination in ordinary life . . . is to produce, out of the society we have to live in, a vision of the society we want to live in" (1964, 140). Economists preach ethics unaware, but have limited their imagination in the telling of ethical stories.

Economics seems to be ready to turn back to some ethical thinking. Many economists have realized the utilitarian hat does not have a rabbit inside. Economics requires ethical thinking in detail, and ethical thinking requires stories, the imagination exercised through time. A proper *homo economicus* recognizes that he is *homo narrans,* a teller of stories and a conveyer of character, and therefore, as Booth points out, *homo iudicans.* When he catches on he'll make better company to keep.

11 The Common Weal and
and Economic Stories

*T*he worldly philosophers change the world with their stories and metaphors. There's work for the econo-literary critic in showing how the rhetoric matters to policy and in distinguishing the good stories of policy from the bad. (Robert Boynton, among other things a politico-literary critic, has done so for the Senate Agriculture Committee [1987].)

The stories in economics are numerous beyond count. The moral outrage that fuels some of them is surprising in so desiccated a science. Since its beginnings economics has reserved its second greatest indignation for monopolists (its first greatest is for clumsy governments). When most economists think of American doctors, for example, they think of monopoly. On the face of it the analogy does not look persuasive. After all, there are hundreds of thousands of doctors, not one, so in no literal sense does the medical profession constitute one seller. Medicine talks about itself in noncommercial terms, as a disinterested science and a sacrificing profession. The economists see it differently, largely because of the story they tell (see McCloskey 1985b, 345). Once upon a time (namely, until the 1930s) medical doctors in the United States earned roughly the same as lawyers or middle management. Then, beginning about 1910 and concluding by about World War II, through their state boards of medical examiners and the corruption of state legislatures, the doctors seized control of the supply of health care, closing medical schools, forbidding foreign doctors to immigrate, and preventing nurses, pharmacists, and others from

150

practicing medicine, at just the time that medicine began to cure more people than it killed. The result was an astonishing increase in the relative income of American doctors (not matched in places like Britain or Italy where the doctors did not succeed in blockading entry), who now earn three times what comparable professionals earn, happily ever after. The economist views the behavior of the American Medical Association as union power more effective than that of plumbers and electricians, concealed behind a myth of self-sacrifice and a facade of ethical purpose. The economic story results in shockingly harsh ethical judgments about the American doctor. A bus driver, says the economist, holds the lives of more people in his hands; a lawyer works longer hours; a professor studies more. But the doctor exploits the most tax shelters, putting medical care out of the reach of the poor.

Economists have developed over the past twenty years or so a similar story about regulation, which, like the medical story, they teach to their students as gospel (291). What is notable is the change in attitude. Economists once retold the Progressive story, assuming without irony that regulators would be able to defy politics for the good of the community. Prohibition, the city manager movement, and especially the regulation of monopoly were all favorites of American economists in the first two decades of the century. The Progressive program was of course put into practice by the New Deal and by the Great Society programs of the 1960s. But since those Progressive times the economists have changed their story.

In the new story, the Interstate Commerce Commission, for example, is said to have been taken over by the very railroads it was supposed to regulate shortly after its formation in 1887 (and later by the big trucking firms). The hero of the Progressive story, a selfless regulator protecting the little man from big business, has for two decades raised increasingly derisive laughter in the halls of economics departments. The economist asks with a smirk: "Do you really expect United Van Lines to sit idly by while the ICC guts its profit?" The moral authority of one regulatory commission after another has been undermined in the eyes of economists by the new story line (lately, for example, the Securities and Exchange Commission, by Phillips and Zecher 1981). The results show in deregulation, an example of the power of ideas as against vested interests. Ideas, not dollars, conquered the regulatory agencies. Many of the agencies were in fact infiltrated by economists educated at universities like Chicago and UCLA, which had long been telling the anti-regulatory tale. The economist's story has become the law.

The story of monopoly, to take a related example, was told for a long time in economics as a story of "structure, conduct, and performance." That is, monopoly was viewed as rain, some of which must fall upon each society. Markets came with "structures" of one seller or two sellers or many sellers, causeless and natural. The job of the economist was to provide umbrellas for the victims of the bad performance. Until the 1970s every course outside the University of Chicago and a few other places in "industrial organization" (the field of economics that studies monopoly and competition) told this tale: monopoly just happens and the economist just stops it. Since the 1970s a new and richer story of monopoly has been told, of how a monopoly comes to be a monopoly, and what therefore is to be done about each separate history. The new theories are casuistical, argued case by case under principles that cannot be applied as invariant rules. If a monopoly of computers arises from one of many potential competitors, for example, it may not be desirable to regulate it, since the disciplining threat of new entry remains.

The analogous case is slum clearance, a long-standing policy of enlightened nations. Slums are bad relative to ideal communities, of course, just as a monopoly is bad relative to an ideal industry. The instinct of the social engineer is therefore to clear the slums and break up the monopoly. But the result has commonly been the concentration of the poor into housing projects worse than the original slums, and the concentration of political pressure into regulatory commissions more monopolistic than the monopolies.

The causes of slums reassert themselves in the Robert Taylor Homes along the Dan Ryan Expressway in Chicago, since the housing was not itself a cause. So too in the regulation of monopoly: when monopoly is caused by the exercise of political power, as it often is, putting politics in charge of the industry is not going to help. The political economy asserts itself in the golden rule, that those who have the gold, rule.

The stories of economics matter to all manner of economic policy. Consider the story of helping poor countries, whose minimal plot is: Once the poor countries were poor, then the rich countries helped them, and now they too are rich. Peter Bauer, an Austrian-British economist who has long criticized the ruling metaphors in this story, has now the satisfaction of seeing his grimmest prediction come true (1984). As he feared some decades ago the advice of economists has on balance hurt the poor countries of the world, hurting more as the quarrel over equality between "The North" and "The South" has intensified. Most of the followers have moved along the track, but notably slower than the leaders.

It is not surprising that an economics taking itself to be value-free social engineering should do a poor job in advising poor countries. Economics around 1950 gave up social philosophy and social history to become a blackboard subject. The poor countries provided convenient laboratories to try out what was discovered on the blackboard. The governments of Western Europe proved wary of the snake oil, but other governments, and intergovernmental governments, lined up at the wagon to buy.

The result was a devaluation by intellectuals of voluntary exchange. After all, what is so fine about voluntary exchange if crushing it can produce the wealth of nations? And why should historical and philosophical doubts that the wealth arises from planning be entertained if a sweet diagram can prove that planning works? The planning and government programs worked badly, on the whole, as is suggested by the unraveling of Eastern Europe and the stagnation of South Asia and the long night of Africa. The postwar experiment with planning was a treason of the clerks, arising from their religion, an irrational belief in their ability to predict and control.

The metaphor of the "Third World" itself was born (as Bauer has noted) with foreign aid and anti-communism shortly after the war. It asks a question of equity. Is it fair that the First World has all the riches? By the mere act of speaking of equity versus efficiency the economists import into the argument, as though it was uncontroversial, a utilitarian ethic. The audience is invited to think of tradeoffs between the one and the other. As the economists would say, mathproudly, $U = U$ (Efficiency, Equity), in which Efficiency is the size of national income and Equity is measured by the distribution of income. This is not "wrong"; it is simply one metaphor among many, some more apt for particular uses than others. If economists think of equity in such terms, for example, they will not ask how the Efficiency was achieved (by executing people jailed in football stadiums, say) or whether Equity entails stealing from innocents (by executing people who buy low and sell high).

The North is meant to feel guilty that by the grace of God it gets more than the South. Bauer has treated at length (1984, chap. 5) the use of the notion of "our" guilt as a justification for compulsory charity. Clergymen and upper middle class intellectuals delight in the transformation of *mea culpa* into *nostra culpa,* prejudging in a word the weighty question of whether charity should be individual or social.

Bauer notes similarly the danger in the related metaphor of "nation building," a handsome neoclassical building in which political prisoners scream in the basement. The figure of a building treats people as "lifeless bricks, to be moved by some master builder" (5). Nation building is not merely a metaphor, mere ornamental rhetoric, but a political argument put into a word. The "nation" is to be "built" by the government, indeed by the present set of colonels and chieftains in charge of the building project.

The very word "development" is a metaphor, of course, limiting our thinking at the same time it makes thinking possible. "Economic growth" sounds better than "economic change," and "change" better than "losing existing jobs," but they are translatable one into the other, suggesting different policies. Economists are not usually conscious of the difference the words make. A self-conscious metaphor has a different effect from an unself-conscious one. The economist and social thinker Mancur Olson has used comparisons among one-man boats, eight-man boats, and multi-oared galleys to illuminate the wealth of nations (Olson 1987). He uses the figure openly and self-consciously, and therefore the effect is merely communicative and ornamental. An explicit metaphor does not bite.

The word "problem," likewise, answers an economic question before one thinks to ask it. Many reputable economists argue for example that the balance-of-payments "problem" is not a problem at all, in the sense of something requiring that "we" find "a solution." No one would worry about the balance of payments if the statistics on it were not collected—which is not something that can be said about some other problems facing an economic community, such as poverty or inflation. Yet many people are exercised about The Problem and propose desperate remedies. The statistics led the British government during the 1950s and early 1960s to a policy of "stop-go," with lurching booms and governmentally-induced busts, damaging the British economy for the long run.

The nineteenth century invented the talk of a "social *problem,*" an "economic *problem,*" and the like, problems which finally the Great Geometer in London or Washington is to solve with compass and straightedge. The economic historian Max Hartwell speaks often of the rhetoric of British parliamentary inquiries in the nineteenth century as defining problems where no one had seen them before. It is not always done with mirrors, of course; this or that condition worthy of correction does exist. But in any case it is done with words. Someone who has persuaded you to speak of inequality of income as a problem has accomplished the most difficult part of her task.

In particular, the array of metaphors taken from sport are crucial to the solving of problems. Sporting metaphors present themselves as innocuous ornaments and are especially popular among Americans, who, goodhearted as they are, favor the happy notion that in a conflict no one really gets hurt (Europeans will use metaphors of war and conquest in similar cases). The ideal is team play, joining together to score a goal against the foreigner or in a more mellow way to "achieve a personal goal." Whenever we hear that "we" should do such and such the signal has been raised: watch for the team metaphor in action.

The best that human frailty is likely to achieve along this line is a book on *The Zero-Sum Solution: Building a World-Class American Economy* (1985) by Lester Thurow, an economist and dean of the business school at the Massachusetts Institute of Technology. It is an intelligent work from which much can be learned. The book illustrates how much economists agree and how much their agreement depends on their shared devotion to quantitative thinking, the metaphor of a set of accounts.

The trouble lies in its metaphors in aid of storytelling. The book treats income and wealth throughout as being extracted like football yardage from non-Americans, especially Japanese and other Asian non-Americans. "To play a competitive game is not to be a winner—every competitive game has its losers—it is only to be given a chance to win. . . . Free market battles can be lost as well as won, and the United States is losing them on world markets" (59). One chapter is entitled "Constructing an Efficient Team." Thurow talks repeatedly about America "competing" and "beating" the rest of the world with a "world-class economy." At one point he complains that more people do not adopt his favored metaphor, which he calls "reality": "For a society which loves team sports . . . it is surprising that Americans won't recognize the same reality in the far more important international economic game" (107).

In more aggressive moods Thurow trades his football helmet for a flak jacket: "American firms will occasionally be defeated at home and will not have compensating foreign victories" (105). Foreign trade is viewed as the economic equivalent of war. Unsurprisingly, British journalists in the late nineteenth century spoke in identically bellicose terms about the American "threat" and the German "menace." And in part, with due allowance for contingency, the competition for first place on the metaphorical battlefield of commerce led most gratifyingly to the literal battlefields of the Somme and Verdun.

Three metaphors govern Thurow's story: this metaphor of the "international zero-sum game"; a metaphor of the domestic "problem" that damages performance in the game; and a metaphor of "we" who face the problem. We have a domestic *problem* of productivity that leads to a *loss* in the international *game*. Thurow has spent a long time interpreting the world with these linked metaphors (he has written other books using them, as have many journalists: Thurow is unusual only in being a good economist using such rhetoric). It is America's job to "compete on world markets" (48), not to make itself wise and competent; what "counts" in Japanese economic performance are its export industries (49), not its wretchedly inefficient agriculture and retailing.

The subject, though, is the exchange of goods and services, Japanese automobiles for American timber, German steel tubes for Soviet natural gas. The game metaphor does not seem apt. If exchange is a game it resembles one in which everyone wins, like aerobic dancing. Trade in this view is *not* zero sum. It is positive sum. There are social, overall, mutual gains from trade. How does an economist know? Because the trade was voluntary. That's Adam Smith's metaphor.

To be sure, viewed from the factory floor the trade with Japan (or for that matter with Massachusetts or with the town over the hill) *is* zero sum, which gives Thurow's metaphor an air of common sense. To a businessperson "fighting" Japanese competition in making automobiles, her loss is indeed Toyota's gain. (Thurow does not view California's competition against Massachusetts with the same alarm. When you think of it, this is strange. If the object is to preserve jobs in Massachusetts, then assembly plants in California or Tennessee are the main competition, the main taker of jobs, to use the non-economist's way of saying it. Why pick on foreigners?)

The game-playing metaphor looks at only one side of the trade, the selling side. As Adam Smith remarked famously, "Consumption is the sole end and purpose of all production; and the interest of the producer ought to be attended to, only so far as it may be necessary for promoting that of the consumer" (1976 [1776], 179). Economists claim to see around and underneath the economy. They claim to do the accounts from the social point of view. Underneath it all (again: the economist's favorite metaphor) Jim Beam of Iowa trades with Tatsuro Saki of Tokyo. A Toyota sold to the United States pays for 2,000 tons of soybeans bought by Japan. The mainstream economist's metaphor of mutual trade differs from that of the anti-economic economists, such as Friedrich List, the German theorist of the *Zollverein,* or Henry Carey, the American theorist of protection in the nineteenth century, or Lester Thurow.

"The heart of America's competitiveness problem is to be found in low productivity growth. . . . [Well-wishers of America] would have to advocate some form of industrial policy to cure the competitiveness problem" (100–01). Problems have solutions, called "policies," which "we must adopt." It is not hard to guess who the Solver is: I'm from the Government, and I'm here to solve your problem. The confidence in the ideas of economists and planners is hardly justified by experience. Do economists really know enough that planning for research and development, in imitation of the Japanese, should be handed over to a MITI-ish organization? Thurow speaks repeatedly of "social organization": we can do better by conscious planning, says he, and of course we know the group of experts who should do the planning.

Thurow's metaphor gets its appeal from the story into which it fits. The story is the one imposed on late Victorian Britain: in the sunset of hegemony, Britain basked complacently while others hustled. American intellectuals are worried that something similar is about to happen to them. The same reply can be made: American income after all will continue to grow whether or not America continues to have the literal lead in income. (In any case, American growth has been slower than that of most countries for most of its history: like Britain, it started rich.)

And why would one wish American hegemony to be fastened on the world forever? Is it God's plan that the United States of America should ever after be Top Nation? Why should we wish relative poverty in perpetuity on our Chinese and Latin American friends? Is this what economic ethics leads us to? It is a finding of economic history that trade among rich nations is better for the rich nations than trade with poor countries (McCloskey 1981, chap. 9). In any case, one would think that the proper audience for policy would be a citizen of the world, not merely an American. What does it matter to me if my relatively wealthy neighbor in Virginia chooses to read too few good books? Shouldn't I care more about the appalling poverty of people in Bangladesh?

The answer is not obvious one way or the other. The claims of community have to be taken seriously. The appropriateness of a strictly nationalist rhetoric for policy, however, is seldom questioned. What is the ethically relevant community? Some years ago at the Institute for Advanced Study at Princeton the political scientist Joseph Carens gave a luncheon talk about his research on American immigration policy. The audience expected him to say that concerning illegal immigration We Have a Problem—namely, how to prevent it without adopting too obviously barbarous measures—because that was the line among megalopolitan intellectuals, raised to believe that trade unions and progressiveness are one. Instead he argued that Mexicans who come to America to better themselves, even if they hurt some workers with American passports, have equal claim to our ethical concern as people born north of the Rio Grande. To the audience at Princeton it was a startling idea, that the egalitarian ethic should extend to the wretchedly poor across the border. The shock in those liberal halls of intellectual power was palpable. People were embarrassed that someone had spoken against nationalism in ethics. It was evident that stories and metaphors about immigration, which spoke of good unions undermined by foreign scabs, were largely unexamined.

Talk of America's problem with foreign competition entails a bitter nationalism. The nationalistic, game-playing (and warmongering) stories can fit with any sort of economics. Linked with socialism, they become national socialism, the better to protect the fatherland, or socialism in one country, the better to protect the motherland. Linked with laissez faire, they become imperialism, the better to protect United Fruit. As Smith said in 1776, "A great empire has been established for the sole purpose of raising up a nation of customers who should be obliged to buy from the shops of our different producers" (Bk. IV, chap. viii; Cannan, 2:180). None of these can be the intent of Thurow and the anti-immigrationists and the other enthusiasts for protection and industrial planning. All the more reason to examine soberly their metaphors and stories.

The Productivity Problem in recent American history is not a figment. Americans are for instance alarmingly badly educated, considering their incomes (for which we professors, incidentally, need to take some blame). Maybe such embarrassment is to be expected out of the great experiment of getting along without an aristocracy. Tocqueville thought so, and he was often right. But in any case productivity has nothing to do with international competitiveness and the balance of payments. As your local economist will be glad to make clear, the pattern of trade depends on comparative advantage, not absolute advantage. That Michael Jordan can do everything with a basketball does not suggest a policy of having the rest of his team sit down. That some country—say, the fabled America of yore, "dominant" in world manufacturing— can do both agriculture and manufacturing better than anyone else does not suggest a policy of making it do everything and import nothing. The overall level of productivity has no effect on America's trade balance. None. And the trade balance is not a measure of excellence. None. The two having nothing to do with each other. We could achieve an enormous and positive trade balance tomorrow with no pursuit of excellence by forbidding imports. Americans want to trade with Tatsuro, and it makes them better off to do so: that is all.

The idea is not to "compete," whatever that might mean in thrillingly collective policies, but to become skilled and hardworking and therefore rich. Why *foreign* trade should be especially important to the matter is obscure, though speaking against the outlanders is a common topic. The American economy, it happens, has been largely self-sufficient since its beginning, which is no surprise, since it stretches over half a continent. Lester Thurow pooh-poohs as not wealth-producing the "taking in of one's own washing," that is, trading with ourselves. But that is what Americans mainly do and always have done, with good results, thank you very much. The "lost jobs," to repeat, are mainly lost to *domestic* competition.

Like the failed war on poverty and the soon-to-fail war on drugs and the other attempts to arouse "us" to face "our" problems, the national challenge to engage in sporting and more bellicose competition with foreigners is snake oil. If it frightens Americans into investing more in bridges and education maybe it will do some good, by inadvertence. But the danger is using inapt and uncriticized stories and metaphors to rouse us from our slumber. The apter metaphors of economics say this: We do not need to be Number One in order to be happy and prosperous; we do not need to crush the Japanese to keep our self-respect.

So the ethics and policy of economic stories comes round to snake oil again. Eric Hoffer, the San Francisco dock worker and sage, asserted in one of his last books that "The harm done by self-appointed experts in human affairs is usually a product of a priori logic. . . . the logic of events may draw from man's actions consequences which a priori logic cannot foresee" (1979, 26, 28). The distinction Hoffer had in mind is not between logic in the strict sense and events in the strict sense. He was no symbolic logician or runner of controlled experiments. He meant the distinction between metaphors and stories. The *a priori* logic is the extrapolated metaphor, such as the Third World or America's economic game. What we need from our experts is less pretended omniscience and more real wisdom, wisdom to tell the stories testing metaphors and to frame the metaphors that test the stories.

Reunifying some pieces of the conversation of humankind is best tried with hard cases. Economics is a hard case, wrapped in its prideful self-image as Social Physics. The neighbors of economics hate its arrogance, as the neighbors of physics do. If even economics can be shown to be fictional and poetical and historical its story will become better. Its experts will stop terrorizing the neighborhood and peddling snake oil. Technically speaking the economist's story will become, as it should, a useful comedy— comprising words of wit, amused tolerance for human folly, stock characters colliding at last in the third act, and, most characteristic of the genre, a universe in equilibrium and a happy ending.

"Now, Herbie," I say, "I do not doubt your information, because I know you will not give out information unless it is well founded. But," I say, "I seldom stand for a tip, and as for betting fifty for you, you know I will not bet fifty even for myself if somebody guarantees me a winner. So I thank you, Herbie, just the same," I say, "but I must do without your tip," and with this I start walking away.

"Now," Herbie says, "wait a minute. A story goes with it," he says.

Well, of course this is a different matter entirely.

Damon Runyon, "A Story Goes with It," *A Treasury of Damon Runyon* (NY: Modern Library, 1958), 152

Works Cited

Abrams, M. H. 1981. *A Glossary of Literary Terms.* 4th ed. NY: Holt, Rinehart and Winston.

Adams, Henry. 1931 [1906]. *The Education of Henry Adams.* NY: Modern Library.

Allen, Robert C. 1979. International Competition in Iron and Steel, 1850–1913. *Journal of Economic History* 39 (December): 911–37.

Austen, Jane. 1965. [1818]. *Persuasion.* NY: Houghton Mifflin.

Austin, J. L. 1975 [1962]. *How to Do Things with Words.* Cambridge, Mass.: Harvard University Press.

Bauer, Peter. 1984. *Reality and Rhetoric: Studies in the Economics of Development.* Cambridge, Mass.: Harvard University Press.

Bazerman, Charles. 1987. Codifying the Social Scientific Style: The APA *Publication Manual* as Behaviorist Rhetoric. In *The Rhetoric of the Human Sciences,* 125–44. *See* Nelson, Megill, and McCloskey, eds., 1987.

————. 1988. *Shaping Written Knowledge: The Genre and the Activity of the Experimental Article in Science.* Madison: University of Wisconsin Press, in the series The Rhetoric of the Human Sciences.

Bely, Andrey. 1985 [1909]. The Magic of Words. In *Selected Essays of Andrey Bely,* 93–104. Translated by S. Cassedy. Berkeley and Los Angeles: University of California Press.

Billig, Michael. 1989. Psychology, Rhetoric, and Cognition. *History of the Human Sciences* 2 (October): 289–307.

Bishop, Errett. 1985. *Constructive Analysis.* Berlin and NY: Springer-Verlag.

Black, Max. 1962. *Models and Metaphors.* Ithaca: Cornell University Press.

Bloom, Allan. 1970. An Interpretation of Plato's *Ion. Interpretation* 1 (Summer): 43–62. Reprinted in Thomas Pangle, ed., *Roots of Political*

Philosophy: Ten Forgotten Socratic Dialogues, 371–95. Ithaca: Cornell University Press, 1987.

Bloom, Harold. 1976. *Wallace Stevens: The Poems of Our Climate.* Ithaca: Cornell University Press.

Booth, Wayne C. 1974. *Modern Dogma and the Rhetoric of Assent.* Chicago: University of Chicago Press.

————. 1988. *The Company We Keep: An Ethics of Fiction.* Berkeley and Los Angeles: University of California Press.

Boswell, James. 1949 [1791]. *The Life of Samuel Johnson, LL. D.* Everyman's Library, in two vols. Vol. 1. London: Dent.

Boynton, G. R. 1987. Telling a Good Story: Models of Argument, Models of Understanding in the Senate Agriculture Committee. In Joseph W. Wenzel, ed., *Argument and Critical Practices,* 429–38. Annandale, VA: Speech Communication Association.

Bridbury, A. R. 1975. *Economic Growth: England in the Later Middle Ages.* Brighton: Harvester.

Brier, Bob. 1980. *Ancient Egyptian Magic.* NY: Morrow.

Brooks, Peter. 1985. *Reading for the Plot: Design and Intention in Narrative.* NY: Vintage.

Bruner, Jerome. 1986. *Actual Minds, Possible Worlds.* Cambridge, Mass.: Harvard University Press.

Bruns, Gerald L. 1984. The Problem of Figuration in Antiquity. In G. Shapiro and A. Sica, eds., *Hermeneutics: Questions and Prospects,* 147–64. Amherst: University of Massachusetts Press.

Burk, James. 1988. *Values in the Marketplace: The American Stock Market under Federal Security Law.* Berlin and NY: W. de Gruyter.

Burnham, T. H., and G. O. Hoskins. 1943. *Iron and Steel in Britain, 1870–1930.* London: Allen and Unwin.

Campbell, John Angus. 1987. Charles Darwin: Rhetorician of Science. In *The Rhetoric of the Human Sciences,* 69–86. *See* Nelson, Megill, and McCloskey, eds., 1987.

Carlston, Donal E. 1987. Turning Psychology on Itself: The Rhetoric of Psychology and the Psychology of Rhetoric. In *The Rhetoric of the Human Sciences,* 145–62. *See* Nelson, Megill, and McCloskey, eds., 1987.

Carus-Wilson, E. M. 1954 [1941]. An Industrial Revolution of the Thirteenth Century. *Economic History Review* 2d ser. 11 (1): 39–60. Reprinted in E. M. Carus-Wilson, ed., *Essays in Economic History,* vol. 1, 41–60. London: Edward Arnold.

Clark, Gregory. 1984. Authority and Efficiency: The Labor Market and the Managerial Revolution of the Late Nineteenth Century. *Journal of Economic History* 44 (December): 1069–83.

Clark, Tom. 1978. *The World of Damon Runyon.* NY: Harper and Row.

Coase, R. H. 1988. *The Firm, the Market and the Law.* Chicago: University of Chicago Press.

Cole, Arthur H. 1953 [1946]. An approach to the Study of Entrepreneurship. *Journal of Economic History* 6 (Supplement): 1–15. Reprinted in F. C. Lane and J. C. Riemersma, eds., *Enterprise and Secular Change: Readings in Economic History,* 181–95. Homewood, Ill.: Irwin.

Coleman, D. C. 1977. *The Economy of England 1450–1750.* Oxford: Oxford University Press.

Coleman, Donald, and Christine MacLeod. 1986. Attitudes to New Techniques: British Businessmen, 1800–1950. *Economic History Review* 2d ser. 39 (November): 588–611.

Collins, Harry. 1985. *Changing Order: Replication and Induction in Scientific Practice.* London and Beverly Hills: Sage.

Cootner, P. H., ed. 1964. *The Random Character of Stock Prices.* Cambridge, Mass.: MIT Press.

Cowles, Alfred. 1933. Can Stock Market Forecasters Forecast? *Econometrica* 1 (July): 309–24.

Crafts, N. F. R. 1977. Industrial Revolution in England and France: Some Thoughts on the Question "Why was England First?" *Economic History Review* 2d ser. 30 (August): 429–41.

———. 1984. *Economic Growth During the British Industrial Revolution.* Oxford: Oxford University Press.

Cunningham, J. V. 1976. *The Collected Essays of J. V. Cunningham.* Chicago: The Swallow Press.

Davis, Philip J., and Reuben Hersh. 1987. Rhetoric and Mathematics. In *The Rhetoric of the Human Sciences,* 53–68. *See* Nelson, Megill, and McCloskey, eds., 1987.

Defoe, Daniel. 1975 [1719]. *Robinson Crusoe.* Edited by Michael Shinagel. Norton Critical Edition. NY: Norton.

Elbaum, Bernard, and William Lazonick, eds. 1986. *The Decline of the British Economy.* NY: Oxford University Press.

Elster, Jon. 1978. *Logic and Society: Contradictions and Possible Worlds.* NY: Wiley.

Euripides. *Hecuba.* Translated by W. Arrowsmith. In *Euripides III: Four Tragedies.* Chicago: University of Chicago Press, 1958.

———. *Iphigenia in Aulis.* Translated by W. Bynner. In *Euripides IV: Four Tragedies.* Chicago: University of Chicago Press, 1958.

Fenoaltea, S. n.d. *Italian Industrial Production, 1861–1913: A Statistical Reconstruction.* Cambridge: Cambridge University Press. Forthcoming.

Fogel, Robert W. 1964. *Railroads and American Economic Growth: Essays in Econometric History.* Baltimore: Johns Hopkins University Press.

————. 1979. Notes on the Social Saving Controversy. *Journal of Economic History* 39 (March): 1–54.

————. 1989. *Without Consent or Contract: The Rise and Fall of American Slavery.* NY: Norton.

Frye, Northrop. 1957. *An Anatomy of Criticism.* NY: Athenaeum.

————. 1964. *The Educated Imagination.* Bloomington: Indiana University Press.

Fussell, Paul. 1979. *Poetic Meter and Poetic Form.* Rev. ed. NY: Random House.

Galison, Peter. 1987. *How Experiments End.* Chicago: University of Chicago Press.

Geertz, Clifford. 1988. *Works and Lives: The Anthropologist as Author.* Stanford: Stanford University Press.

Gergen, Kenneth J., and Mary M. Gergen. 1986. Narrative Form and the Construction of Psychological Science. In T. R. Sarbin, ed., *Narrative Psychology: The Storied Nature of Human Conduct,* 22–44. NY: Praeger.

Gerschenkron, Alexander. 1952. Economic Backwardness in Historical Perspective. Reprinted in *Economic Backwardness,* 5–30. *See* Gerschenkron 1962d.

————. 1962a. On The Concept of Continuity in History. Reprinted in *Continuity,* 11–39. *See* Gerschenkron 1968.

————. 1962b. The Typology of Industrial Development as a Tool of Analysis. Reprinted in *Continuity,* 77–97. *See* Gerschenkron 1968.

————. 1962c. The Approach to European Industrialization: A postscript. In *Economic Backwardness,* 353–66. *See* Gerschenkron 1962d.

————. 1962d. *Economic Backwardness in Historical Perspective: A Book of Essays.* Cambridge, Mass.: Harvard University Press.

————. 1965. Foreword. In Albert Fishlow, *American Railroads and the Transformation of the Ante-Bellum Economy.* Cambridge, Mass.: Harvard University Press.

————. 1968. *Continuity in History and Other Essays.* Cambridge, Mass.: Harvard University Press.

————. 1970. *Europe in the Russian Mirror: Four Lectures on Economic History.* Cambridge: Cambridge University Press.

————. 1977. *An Economic Spurt That Failed: Four Lectures in Austrian History.* Princeton: Princeton University Press.

Gibson, Walker. 1980 [1950]. Authors, Speakers, and Mock Readers. *College English* 11 (February). Reprinted in Jane P. Tompkins, ed., *Reader-Response Criticism*, 1–6. Baltimore: Johns Hopkins University Press.

Goodman, Nelson. 1965. *Fact, Fiction and Forecast.* 2d ed. Indianapolis: Bobbs-Merrill.

————. 1978. *Ways of Worldmaking.* Indianapolis: Hackett.

Gould, Stephen Jay. 1987. *Time's Arrow, Time's Cycle: Myth and Metaphor in the Discovery of Geological Time.* Cambridge, Mass.: Harvard University Press.

————. 1989. *Wonderful Life: The Burgess Shale and the Nature of History.* NY: Norton.

Greene, Thomas M. 1989. The Poetics of Discovery: A Reading of Donne's Elegy 19. *Yale Journal of Criticism* 2(2):129–43.

Haddock, David D. 1986. First Possession versus Optimal Timing: Limiting the Dissipation of Economic Value. *Washington University Law Quarterly* 64 (Fall): 775–92.

Harley, C. K. 1982. British Industrialization before 1841: Evidence of Slower Growth during the Industrial Revolution. *Journal of Economic History* 42 (June): 267–90.

Hartwell, R. M. 1967 [1965]. The Causes of the Industrial Revolution: An Essay in Methodology. *Economic History Review* 2d ser. 18 (August): 164–82. Reprinted in R. M. Hartwell, ed., *The Causes of the Industrial Revolution in England*, 53–80. London: Methuen.

Heinzelman, Kurt. 1980. *The Economics of the Imagination.* Amherst: University of Massachusetts Press.

Hexter, J. H. 1986. The Problem of Historical Knowledge. Washington University, St. Louis. Typescript.

Higgs, Robert. 1987. *Crisis and Leviathan: Critical Episodes in the Growth of American Government.* NY: Oxford University Press.

Hirschman, Albert O. 1970. The Search for Paradigms as a Hindrance to Understanding. *World Politics* 22 (March). Reprinted in P. Rabinow and W. M. Sullivan, eds., *Interpretive Social Science: A Reader,* 163–79. Berkeley and Los Angeles: University of California Press, 1979.

Hoffer, Eric. 1979. *Before the Sabbath.* NY: Harper and Row.

Iser, Wolfgang. 1980. The Interaction between Text and Reader. In Susan R. Suleiman and Inge Crosman, eds., *The Reader in the Text: Essays on Audience and Interpretation,* 106–19. Princeton: Princeton University Press, 1980.

Jonsen, Albert R., and Stephen Toulmin. 1988. *The Abuse of Casuistry: A*

History of Moral Reasoning. Berkeley and Los Angeles: University of California Press.

Keegan, John. 1978 [1976]. *The Face of Battle.* Harmondsworth, Middlesex: Penguin.

Kennedy, George A. 1984. *New Testament Interpretation through Rhetorical Criticism.* Chapel Hill: University of North Carolina Press.

Kennedy, William P. 1982. Economic Growth and Structural Change in the United Kingdom, 1870–1914. *Journal of Economic History* 42 (March): 105–14.

Kenner, Hugh. 1987. *Magic and Spells (About Curses, Charms and Riddles).* Bennington Chapbooks in Literature, Ben Belitt Lectureship Series. Bennington, VT.

Kingsland, Sharon E. 1985. *Modeling Nature: Episodes in the History of Population Ecology.* Chicago: University of Chicago Press.

Klamer, Arjo. 1983. *Conversations with Economists: New Classical Economists and Opponents Speak Out on the Current Controversy in Macroeconomics.* Totowa, NJ: Rowman and Allanheld.

———. 1987a. As If Economists and Their Subjects Were Rational. In *Rhetoric of the Human Sciences,* 163–83. *See* Nelson, Megill, and McCloskey, eds., 1987.

———. 1987b. The Advent of Modernism in Economics. University of Iowa. Typescript.

Klamer, Arjo, Donald N. McCloskey, Robert M. Solow, eds. 1988. *The Consequences of Economic Rhetoric.* NY: Cambridge University Press.

Korner, S. 1967. Continuity. In *The Encyclopedia of Philosophy.* NY: Macmillan and Free Press.

Landau, Misia. 1987. Paradise Lost: The Theme of Terrestiality in Human Evolution. In *The Rhetoric of the Human Sciences,* 111–24. *See* Nelson, Megill, and McCloskey, eds., 1987.

Landes, David. 1969. *The Unbound Prometheus: Technological Change and Industrial Development in Western Europe from 1750 to the Present.* Cambridge: Cambridge University Press. (Reprinting with additions his book-length essay Technological Change and Development in Western Europe, 1750–1914 in *The Cambridge Economic History of Europe,* Vol. 6. Cambridge: Cambridge University Press, 1965.)

Lavoie, Don. 1985. *Rivalry and Central Planning: The Socialist Calculation Debate Reconsidered.* Cambridge: Cambridge University Press.

Lazonick, William. 1987. Stubborn Mules: Some Comments. *Economic History Review* 2d ser. 40 (February): 80–86.

Levinson, Stephen C. 1983. *Pragmatics*. Cambridge: Cambridge University Press.

Levy, David. 1989. *The Economic Ideas of Ordinary People*. Department of Economics, George Mason University. Book manuscript.

Lewis, C. S. 1962 [1939]. Buspels and Flansferes: A Semantic Nightmare. In his *Rehabilitations and Other Essays*. Reprinted in Max Black, ed., *The Importance of Language*. Englewood Cliffs, NJ: Prentice-Hall.

Lillo, George. 1952 [1731]. The London Merchant. In Ricardo Quintana ed., *Eighteenth-Century Plays*. NY: Modern Library.

Lindert, Peter H., and Keith Trace. 1971. Yardsticks for Victorian Entrepreneurs. In Donald N. McCloskey, ed., *Essays on a Mature Economy: Britain after 1840*, 239–74. London: Methuen.

McClelland, Peter D. 1975. *Causal Explanation and Model Building in History, Economics, and the New Economic History*. Ithaca: Cornell University Press.

McCloskey, D. N. 1970. Britain's Loss from Foreign Industrialization: A Provisional Estimate. *Explorations in Economic History* 8 (Winter): 141–52.

————. 1971. [with Lars G. Sandberg] From Damnation to Redemption: Judgments on the Victorian Entrepreneur. *Explorations in Economic History* 9 (Fall): 89–108.

————. 1973. *Economic Maturity and Entrepreneurial Decline: British Iron and Steel, 1870–1913*. Cambridge, Mass.: Harvard University Press.

————. 1979. No It Did Not: A Reply to Craft's Comment on "Did Victorian Britain Fail?" *Economic History Review* 2d ser. 32 (Nov): 538–41.

————. 1981. *Enterprise and Trade in Victorian Britain: Essays in Historical Economics*. London: Allen and Unwin.

————. 1985a. *The Rhetoric of Economics*. Madison: University of Wisconsin Press, in the series The Rhetoric of the Human Sciences.

————. 1985b. *The Applied Theory of Price*. NY: Macmillan.

McGrath, Francis C. 1986. *The Sensible Spirit: Walter Pater and the Modernist Paradigm*. Tampa: University of South Florida Press.

MacIntyre, Alasdair. 1981. *After Virtue*. Notre Dame, Ind.: University of Notre Dame Press.

McKeon, Richard. 1987. *Rhetoric: Essays in Invention and Discovery*. Woodbridge, Conn.: The Ox Bow Press.

McPherson, James M. 1988. *The Battle Cry of Freedom*. NY: Oxford University Press.

Maddison, Angus. 1989. *The World Economy in the Twentieth Century.* Paris: Development Centre of the Organization for Economic Co-operation and Development.

Madison, G. B. 1982. *Understanding: A Phenomenological-Pragmatic Analysis.* Westport, Conn.: Greenwood Press.

Malkiel, Burton. 1985. *A Random Walk Down Wall Street.* 4th ed. NY: Norton.

Mantoux, Paul. 1961 [1928]. *The Industrial Revolution in the Eighteenth Century.* NY: 1961.

Marshall, Alfred. 1890. *Principles of Economics.* London: Macmillan.

Martin, Wallace. 1986. *Recent Theories of Narrative.* Ithaca: Cornell University Press.

Mauss, Marcel. 1972 [1902–03]. *A General Theory of Magic.* NY: Norton.

Medawar, Peter. 1964. Is the Scientific Paper Fraudulent? *Saturday Review.* 1 August, 42–43.

Megill, Allan, and D. N. McCloskey. 1987. The Rhetoric of History. In *The Rhetoric of the Human Sciences,* 221–38. See Nelson, Megill, and McCloskey, eds., 1987.

Mill, John Stuart. 1872. *A System of Logic.* 8th ed. London: Longmans.

Mokyr, Joel, ed. 1985. *The Economics of the Industrial Revolution.* Totowa, NJ: Rowman and Allanheld.

Montague, F. C. 1900. Morality. In R. H. Palgrave, ed., *Dictionary of Political Economy.* London: Macmillan.

Moore, Ruth. 1985 [1966]. *Niels Bohr.* Cambridge: MIT Press.

Mulkay, Michael. 1985. *The Word and the World: Explorations in the Form of Sociological Analysis.* Winchester, Mass.: Allen and Unwin.

Nash, Christopher, and Martin Warner, eds. 1989. *Narrative in Culture.* London: Routledge.

Nef, J. U. 1932. *The Rise of the British Coal Industry.* 2 vols. London: Routledge.

Nelson, John, Allan Megill, and D. N. McCloskey, eds. 1987. *The Rhetoric of the Human Sciences: Language and Argument in Scholarship and Public Affairs.* Madison: University of Wisconsin Press, in the series The Rhetoric of the Human Sciences.

Nicholas, Stephen. 1982. Total Factor Productivity Growth and the Revision of Post-1870 British Economic History. *Economic History Review* 2d ser. 35 (February): 83–98.

———. 1985. British Economic Performance and Total Factor Productivity Growth, 1870–1940. *Economic History Review* 2d ser. 38 (November): 576–82.

Nye, John. 1989. *Lucky Fools*. Department of Economics, Washington University, St. Louis. Typescript.

Olson, Mancur. 1963. *The Economics of Wartime Shortage: A History of British Food Supply in the Napoleonic War and in World Wars I and II*. Durham: Duke University Press.

————. 1987. Diseconomies of Scale and Development. *Cato Journal* 7 (Spring/Summer): 77–98.

Oxford. 1933. *The Oxford English Dictionary*, vol. 9, S–Soldo. Oxford: Clarendon Press.

————. 1982. *A Supplement to the Oxford English Dictionary*, vol. 3, O–Scz. Oxford: Clarendon Press.

————. 1989. *The Oxford English Dictionary*. 2d ed. Vol. 14, Rob–Sequyle. Oxford: Clarendon Press.

Payne, Peter. 1978. Industrial Leadership and Management in Great Britain. In P. Mathias and M. M. Postan, eds., *The Cambridge Economic History of Europe*, vol. 7, pt. 1, 180–230. Cambridge: Cambridge University Press.

Perelman, Chaim. 1982. *The Realm of Rhetoric*. Notre Dame, Ind.: University of Notre Dame Press.

Perelman, Chaim, and L. Olbrechts-Tyteca. 1969 [1958]. *The New Rhetoric: A Treatise on Argumentation*. Translated by J. Wilkinson and P. Weaver. Notre Dame, Ind.: University of Notre Dame Press.

Phillips, Susan M., and J. Richard Zecher. 1981. *The SEC and the Public Interest*. Cambridge, Mass.: MIT Press.

Plato. *Cratylus*. Translated by H. N. Fowler. Loeb Series. London and NY: Heinemann and Putnam, 1926.

Prince, Gerald. 1973. *A Grammar of Stories*. The Hague and Paris: Mouton.

Propp, Vladímir. 1968. [1928]. *Morphology of the Folktale*. 2d ed. Translated by L. Scott and L. A. Wagner. American Folklore Society. Austin: University of Texas Press.

Rabinowitz, Peter J. 1980 [1968]. "What's Hecuba to Us?" The Audience's Experience of Literary Borrowing. In Susan R. Suleiman and Inge Crosman, eds., *The Reader in the Text: Essays on Audience and Interpretation*, 241–63. Princeton: Princeton University Press.

Redlich, Fritz. 1970 [1968]. Potentialities and Pitfalls in Economic History. *Explorations in Entrepreneurial History* 2d ser. 6 (1): 93–108. Reprinted in R. L. Andreano, ed., *The New Economic History*. NY: Wiley.

Rosaldo, Renato. 1987. Where Objectivity Lies: The Rhetoric of Anthropology. In *The Rhetoric of the Human Sciences,* 87–110. *See* Nelson, Megill, and McCloskey, eds., 1987.

Rosenblatt, Louise M. 1978. *The Reader, the Text, the Poem: The Transactional Theory of the Literary Work.* Carbondale: Southern Illinois University Press.

Rostow, W. W. 1960. *The Stages of Economic Growth.* Cambridge: Cambridge University Press.

Rothenberg, Jerome, ed. 1985. *Technicians of the Sacred.* Berkeley and Los Angeles: University of California Press.

Runyon, Damon. 1958 [1933]. Money From Home. In *A Treasury of Damon Runyon,* 18–32. NY: Modern Library.

Ruthven, K. K. 1979. *Critical Assumptions.* Cambridge: Cambridge University Press.

St. Patrick (attributed). 1947 [c. 440]. Deer's Cry. In Kathleen Hoagland, ed., *1000 Years of Irish Poetry,* 12–14. NY: Devon-Adair.

Samuelson, Paul A. 1986 [1982]. Paul Cootner's Reconciliation of Economic Law with Chance. Reprinted in K. Crowley, ed., *The Collected Scientific Papers of Paul A. Samuelson,* vol. 5, 537–51. Cambridge, Mass.: MIT Press.

Sandberg, Lars G. 1974. *Lancashire in Decline: A Study in Entrepreneurship, Technology, and International Trade.* Columbus: Ohio State University Press.

Santayana, George. 1986 [1943–53]. *Persons and Places.* Vol. 1 of the Works of George Santayana. Cambridge, Mass.: MIT Press.

Sappho. Prayer to Aphrodite. In C. A. Trypanis, ed., *The Penguin Book of Greek Verse,* 144–45. London: Penguin, 1971.

Saussure, F. de. 1983 [1916]. *Course in General Linguistics.* Translated by Roy Harris. London: Duckworth.

Saxonhouse, Gary R., and Gavin Wright. 1984. New Evidence on the Stubborn English Mule and the Cotton Industry, 1878–1920. *Economic History Review* 2d ser. 37 (November): 507–20.

———. 1987. Stubborn Mules and Vertical Integration: The Disappearing Constraint? *Economic History Review* 2d ser. 40 (November): 87–94.

Scholes, Robert, and Robert Kellogg. 1966. *The Nature of Narrative.* London and NY: Oxford University Press.

Schultz, Theodore. 1988. Are University Scholars and Scientists Free Agents? *Southern Humanities Review.* 22 (Summer): 251–60.

Sellar, W. C., and R. J. Yeatman. 1931. *1066 and All That.* NY: Dutton.

Smith, Adam. 1976 [1776]. *An Inquiry into the Nature and Causes of the*

Wealth of Nations. Edited by E. Cannan. Chicago: University of Chicago Press.

Solow, Robert. 1982. Does Economics Make Progress? American Academy of Arts and Sciences, 10 May. Typescript.

Spaziani, Eugene, R. D. Watson, Mark P. Mattson, and Z.-F. Chen. 1989. Ecdysteroid Biosynthesis in the Crustacean Y-Organ and Control by an Eyestalk Neuropeptide. *Journal of Experimental Zoology* 252 (1989): 271–82.

Stevens, Wallace. 1972. *The Palm at the End of the Mind: Selected Poems and a Play.* Edited by Holly Stevens. NY: Vintage.

Tellis, Gerard J. 1988. Advertising Exposure, Loyalty and Brand Purchase: A Two-Stage Model of Choice. *Journal of Marketing Research* 15 (May): 134–144.

Theocritus. II. The Spell. In *The Greek Bucolic Poets,* 24–39. Translated by J. M. Edmonds. London and NY: Heinemann and Putnam, 1923.

Thomas, Keith. 1971. *Religion and the Decline of Magic.* NY: Scribner's.

Thurow, Lester. 1985. *The Zero-Sum Solution: Building a World-Class American Economy.* NY: Simon and Schuster.

Todorov, Tzvetan. 1973/75 [1970]. *The Fantastic: A Structural Approach to a Literary Genre.* Translated by R. Howard. Ithaca: Cornell University Press.

———. 1977 [1971]. *The Poetics of Prose.* Translated by R. Howard. Ithaca: Cornell University Press.

———. 1980 [1975]. Reading as Construction. In R. Suleiman and Inge Crosman, eds., *The Reader in the Text: Essays on Audience and Interpretation,* 67–82. Princeton: Princeton University Press.

———. 1987 (1984). *Literature and Its Theorists: A Personal View of Twentieth-Century Criticism.* Translated by C. Porter. Ithaca: Cornell University Press.

Vickers, Brian. 1988. *In Defense of Rhetoric.* Oxford: Clarendon Press.

Waring, Stephen. n.d. *Beyond Taylorism: An Intellectual History of Business Management since 1946.* Chapel Hill: University of North Carolina Press, forthcoming.

Weinberg, Steven. 1983. Beautiful Theories. Revision of the Second Annual Gordon Mills Lecture on Science and the Humanities, University of Texas, 5 April. Typescript.

Weintraub, E. Roy. 1991. *Stabilizing Dynamics: Constructing Economic Knowledge.* Cambridge: Cambridge University Press.

White, Hayden. 1973. *Metahistory: The Historical Imagination in Nineteenth-Century Europe.* Baltimore: Johns Hopkins University Press.

―――. 1981. The Value of Narrativity in the Representation of Reality. In W. J. T. Mitchell, ed., *On Narrative*, 1–24. Chicago: University of Chicago Press.

Wiener, Martin. 1981. *English Culture and the Decline of the Industrial Spirit, 1850–1980*. Cambridge: Cambridge University Press.

Wilamowitz-Moellendorff, Ulrich von. 1930 [1928]. *My Recollections, 1848–1914*. Translated by G. C. Richards. London: Chatto & Windus.

Williamson, Jeffrey G. 1974. *Late Nineteenth-Century American Development: A General Equilibrium History*. Cambridge: Cambridge University Press.

Woolf, Virginia. 1953 [1925]. *The Common Reader, First Series*. NY and London: Harcourt Brace Jovanovich.

Xenophon. *Memorabilia and Oeconomicus*. Translated by E. C. Marchant. Loeb Series. London and Cambridge: Heinemann and Harvard, 1923.

Zarnowitz, Victor, and Geoffrey Moore. 1982. Sequential Signals of Recession and Recovery. *Journal of Business* 55 (January): 57–85.

Index

177